# Best Practice

## Elementary

## BUSINESS ENGLISH IN CONTEXT

## Coursebook

### BILL MASCULL

**THOMSON** ™

United Kingdom • United States • Australia • Canada • Mexico • Singapore • Spain

# Contents

MODULE

1

INTRODUCTIONS

Meet the people in *Best Practice Elementary*, and the companies they work for.

# 1 Where are you from?

**Listening and speaking**

**A** 🔘 1.1 **Listen and complete.**

1
Hi, my name's Fiona Macpherson. I'm _from_ Scotland.

3
I'm Carole Bruckner. _____ from America.

5
Hi, my _____ Astrid Schmidt. I'm from Frankfurt, in Germany.

2
Hello, I'm Alessandra Tivoli. I'm _____ from Italy.

4
Hello, _____ _____ Saleem Bashir. I'm from Malaysia – Kuala Lumpur.

6
Hello, I'm Sven Karlsson. _____ _____ Sweden, from Uppsala.

**B** 🔘 1.2 **Listen and complete.**

1 I'm _Alessandra Tivoli_ . I'm from Modena, in Italy.
2 I'm _____ _____ . I'm _____ Uppsala, in Sweden.
3 I'm _____ _____ . _____ from Kuala Lumpur, in Malaysia.

**C** 🔘 1.3 **Listen and match the cards to the three conversations.**

a ☐

first name

Splash Pools

**Sven Karlsson**
Sales Manager

146-8 Clapham High St
London SW4 7SS

**Tel** 020 7627 8790
**Fax** 020 7627 8990
**E-mail** sven.karlsson@splashpools.co.uk

family name or surname

b ☐

**KU Industries**
**CAR DIVISION**

201 Jalan Ampang
50450 Kuala Lumpur
Malaysia

t. +60 3 2162 2244
f. +60 3 2162 6829
e. sbashir@kli.com.my

**Saleem Bashir**
Production Engineer

c ☐

**M·C**
Mimosa Cars

Alessandra Tivoli
**Designer**

Via Menotti, 68
41100 Modena, Italy

**Tel:** +39 (0) 59 53 74 21
**Fax:** +39 (0) 59 53 74 60
**E-mail:** alessandra.tivoli@mimosa.it

**Your turn** **D** **Work in pairs. Ask and answer questions in the same way.**

**A:** *Hello. My name's ... Here's my card.*
**B:** *Thank you. Where are you from?*
**A:** *I'm from ...*
**B:** *Nice to meet you.*

## Grammar  *be*

*I'm from Malaysia.*

**A** Complete the table.

| | | |
|---|---|---|
| I'm (I am) | | Malaysia. |
| You're (You are) | | Italy. |
| He's (He is) | | France. |
| _____ (She is) | from | Brazil. |
| We're (We are) | | America. |
| _____ (You are) | | Sweden. |
| _____ (They are) | | Poland. |

■ More information: Grammar overview page 105

▶ More practice: Workbook page 2

**B** 🔘 1.4 Now listen, check and repeat.

## Speaking

**A** Work in pairs. Ask and answer questions about the people in the picture. Use the countries in the box.

> Germany    England    America    Belgium

**A**
1 *Michael Schumacher. Is he from ... ?*
2 *Justine Henin-Hardenne and Kim Clijsters. Are they from ... ?*
3 *Where's he/she from?*
4 *Where are they from?*

**B**
*I don't know. / Yes, he is. / No, he isn't.*
*I don't know. / Yes, they are. / No, they aren't.*

*He's/She's from ...*
*They're from ...*

Michael Schumacher

Tiger Woods

Kim Clijsters and Justine Henin-Hardenne

David Beckham

**Your turn**

**B** Work in pairs. Ask and answer questions about your favourite sportsman and sportswoman and where they are from.

A: *Who's your favourite sportsman?*
B: *Ronaldo.*
A: *Where's he from?*
B: *He's from Brazil.*

A: *Who's your favourite sportswoman?*
B: *Kim Clijsters.*
A: *Where's she from?*
B: *She's from Belgium.*

● More information: Vocabulary builder page 104

## Checklist

✓ say who you are: *I'm Saleem. / My name's Saleem.*

✓ say where you are from: *I'm from Kuala Lumpur.*

✓ ask where someone is from: *Where's she from? – She's from Italy.*

7

**Listening and speaking**

**A** 2.1 **Listen and complete.**

A: *Where's Fiona* <u>from</u> *?*

B: *She's* \_\_\_\_\_ *Scotland.*

A: *What's her* \_\_\_\_\_ *?*

B: *She's* \_\_\_\_\_ *designer.*

**B** **Now listen again and repeat.**

**C** 2.2 **Listen and match the people to their jobs, countries and companies.**

| | | | | | | |
|---|---|---|---|---|---|---|
| Alessandra Tivoli | | Germany. | | a designer | | Splash Pools. |
| Sven Karlsson | is from | Italy. | He's/She's | an engineer | at | KL Industries. |
| Saleem Bashir | | Sweden. | | a sales manager | | Supersport. |
| Astrid Schmidt | | Malaysia. | | a director | | Mimosa Cars. |

**D** **Now say the names of the jobs, the countries and the companies. Then ask and answer questions about the people in pairs.**

A: *Where's Sven from?*

B: *He's from Sweden.*

A: *What's his job?*

B: *He's a sales manager at Splash Pools.*

**Grammar 1** *a/an*

*He's **an** engineer.*

You use:

- *a* or *an* in front of countable nouns.
- *a* in front of nouns that begin with a consonant.   *She's a receptionist.*
- *an* in front of nouns that begin with a vowel.   *He's an artist.*

■ More information: Grammar overview page 111

8

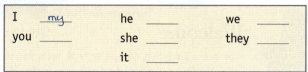

**A  Write *a* or *an*.**

| | | |
|---|---|---|
| 1 _an_ accountant | 3 _____ engineer | 5 _____ sales manager |
| 2 _____ designer | 4 _____ lawyer | 6 _____ personal assistant |

*There are 900,000 lawyers in the US, but only 20,000 in Japan.*

**B  Now listen, check and repeat.**

**Your turn**

**C  Work in pairs. Ask and answer questions about your job.**

A: *What's your job?*

B: *I'm …*

## Grammar 2

### possessive adjectives

*My* name's Astrid.

**A  Complete the table.**

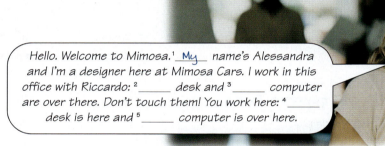

| I | _my_ | he | _____ | we | _____ |
|---|---|---|---|---|---|
| you | _____ | she | _____ | they | _____ |
| | | it | _____ | | |

**B  You have a new job at Mimosa Cars. Alessandra talks to you. Listen and complete.**

> Hello. Welcome to Mimosa. ¹ _My_ name's Alessandra and I'm a designer here at Mimosa Cars. I work in this office with Riccardo: ² _____ desk and ³ _____ computer are over there. Don't touch them! You work here: ⁴ _____ desk is here and ⁵ _____ computer is over here.

■ More information: Grammar overview page 112

## ON THE LINE

**A  Listen and complete.**

| You say: | You hear: |
|---|---|
| *Is Alessandra Tivoli _____ ?* | *Yes, _____ .* |
| *Hello, Alessandra. _____ is Melanie.* | *Hello, _____ .* |

**Your turn**

**B  Work in pairs. Student A looks at this page. Student B looks at page 152.**

**Student A**

Begin three phone calls to:

1 Sven Karlsson

2 Saleem Bashir

3 Astrid Schmidt

## Checklist

✔ job names: an *accountant*, a *receptionist* …

✔ possessive adjectives: *my*, *your* …

✔ ask for someone on the phone and say who you are: *Is Alessandra there? This is Melanie.*

# 3 How many showrooms?

## Reading

**A** Read the website text.

**Splash Pools UK**

**Splash Pools**

**Swedish saunas & pools**

Homepage

Saunas & Pools

Contact us

### Welcome

We are a Swedish company that sells saunas and pools all over Europe. Our head office is in Stockholm, and altogether we have five offices and 14 showrooms in Europe, with 120 employees. Three of the showrooms are in the UK – in London, Bristol and Birmingham. Splash Pools has an office in London. There are 25 employees altogether in the UK.

**B** Now complete the information.

| | | | |
|---|---|---|---|
| 1 In Europe, including the UK | offices __5__ | showrooms _____ | employees _____ |
| 2 In the UK | offices _____ | showrooms _____ | employees _____ |

## Grammar 1

### *be* negative and question forms

***Are you*** from Sweden?

**A** Complete the table.

| | |
|---|---|
| <u>Are</u> you from Argentina? | No, I'<u>m</u> <u>not</u> . I'm from Chile. |
| <u>Is</u> he from Australia? | No, he <u>isn't</u> . He's from New Zealand. |
| _____ she from France? | No, she _____ . She's from Belgium. |
| _____ you from Japan? | No, we _____ . We're from Korea. |
| _____ they from Egypt? | No, they _____ . They're from Tunisia. |

■ More information: Grammar overview page 105

**B** **3.1** Now listen, check and repeat.

## Grammar 2

### *there is; there are; how many*

***There are*** 25 employees in the UK.

**A** Look at the Splash Pools website again and complete the sentences.

1 <u>There's</u> an office in London.
2 _____ there an office in Manchester?   No, there _____ .
3 Are _____ showrooms in Scotland?   No, there _____ .
4 How many showrooms _____ there in England?   There _____ three showrooms.
5 How _____ employees are there in Europe?   There are 120 employees.

▶ More practice: Workbook page 6

**B** **3.2** Now listen, check and repeat.

## Numbers

**A** 🔘 *3.3* **Listen to the numbers and write them down.** 0,

**B** 🔘 *3.4* **Listen to the numbers and circle the ones you hear.**

| | | | | | |
|---|---|---|---|---|---|
| (13) | 30 | 14 | 40 | 15 | 50 |
| 16 | 60 | 17 | 70 | 18 | 80 | 19 | 90 |
| 100 | 125 | 200 | 271 | 333 | 389 | 403 | 499 |

**C** **Match the two parts of the product names. Then match the names to the pictures.**

1 Chanel    a Up

2 7    b 57 varieties

3 Heinz    c no. 5

4 Peugeot    d 747

5 Boeing    e 406

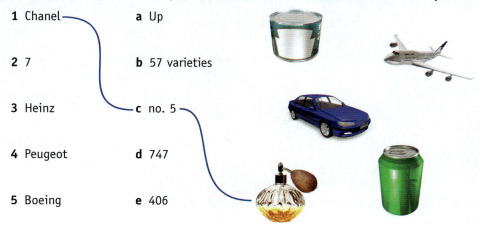

- More information:
  Vocabulary builder
  page 103

**Your turn** **D** **Work in pairs. Student A looks at this page. Student B looks at page 152.**

**Student A**

Ask Student B for the phone numbers for these organisations and write them down.

*What's the number for ... ?*

| | |
|---|---|
| **1** Splash Pools UK _____ | **3** Mimosa Cars _____ |
| **2** Supersport _____ | **4** KL Industries _____ |

## ☎ON THE LINE

**A** 🔘 *3.5* **Listen and complete.**

| You hear: | You say: |
|---|---|
| Hello. | Is that _____ _____ ? |
| Yes, it is. | Can I speak to _____ _____ , please? |
| Who's calling? | |

**Your turn** **B** **Work in pairs. Student A looks at this page. Student B looks at page 152.**

**Student A**

Make three calls and ask for:

1 Astrid Schmidt at Supersport

2 Alessandra Tivoli at Mimosa Cars

3 Saleem Bashir at KL Industries

## Checklist

✓ be negative and question forms: *No, he isn't.*

✓ how many; there is; there are: *How many showrooms are there? – There are 14.*

✓ numbers and phone numbers: *What's the number for ... ?*

✓ ask for someone on the phone: *Can I speak to Sven, please?*

# 4 We make cars

**A** Read the text.

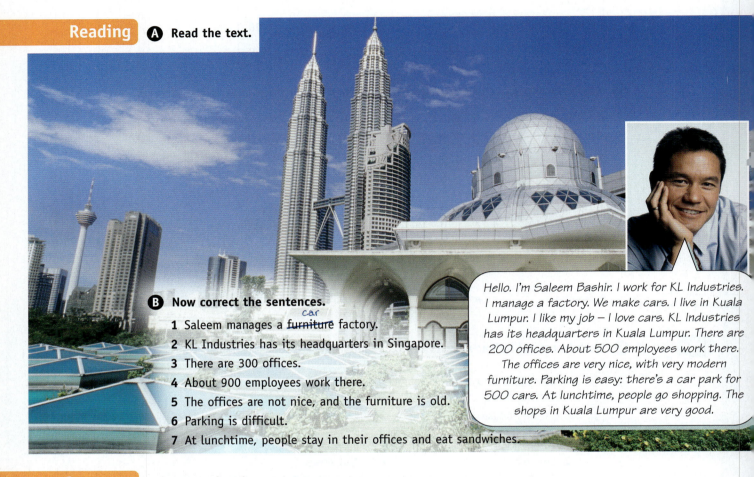

*Hello. I'm Saleem Bashir. I work for KL Industries. I manage a factory. We make cars. I live in Kuala Lumpur. I like my job – I love cars. KL Industries has its headquarters in Kuala Lumpur. There are 200 offices. About 500 employees work there. The offices are very nice, with very modern furniture. Parking is easy: there's a car park for 500 cars. At lunchtime, people go shopping. The shops in Kuala Lumpur are very good.*

**B** Now correct the sentences.

car

1 Saleem manages a ~~furniture~~ factory.
2 KL Industries has its headquarters in Singapore.
3 There are 300 offices.
4 About 900 employees work there.
5 The offices are not nice, and the furniture is old.
6 Parking is difficult.
7 At lunchtime, people stay in their offices and eat sandwiches.

## present simple

*Saleem manage**s** a car factory.*

When you talk about someone, you usually add an *-s* to the base form of the verb.

**A** Complete the table.

| | | |
|---|---|---|
| I work for KL Industries. | → | Saleem _works_ for KL Industries. |
| I manage a car factory. | → | He _____ a car factory. |
| I live in Kuala Lumpur. | → | He _____ in Kuala Lumpur. |
| I like my job. | → | He _____ his job. |
| I love cars. | → | He _____ cars. |

**B** Now listen, check and repeat.

**C** Complete the table.

| | | | |
|---|---|---|---|
| | | speak English? | Yes, I _do_ . |
| | | work in an office? | Yes, I _____ . |
| _____ | you | sell things? | No, I _don't_ . |
| | | manage people? | Yes, I _____ . |
| | | like your job? | Yes, _____ do. |

■ More information: Grammar overview page 105

**D** Now listen, check and repeat.

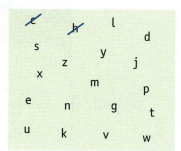

**E** Match the questions to the answers in this interview with Alessandra Tivoli.

1 Do you work in the centre of Modena?
2 Do you make cars?
3 Do you like your work?
4 Do you go shopping at lunchtime?
5 Do you have sandwiches for lunch?

a No, I don't. I have lunch in the company restaurant.
b No, I don't. There are no shops near here.
c No, I don't. I work ten kilometres from the centre.
d No, I don't make cars. I design them.
e Yes, I do. I love my work.

▶ More practice:
Workbook page 8

## Listening

**A** Put the letters into groups that sound the same.

| | | | |
|---|---|---|---|
| a | h | | |
| b | c | | |
| f | | | |
| i | | | |
| o | | | |
| q | | | |
| r | | | |

a̶  h̶  l  d
s  y
z  j
x  m  p
e  n  g  t
u  k  v  w

**B** 🔴 4·3 Now listen and check.

## ⊘N THE LINE

**A** 🔴 4·4 Two people phone Saleem Bashir's personal assistant.
Listen to the two calls and write down their names and contact details.

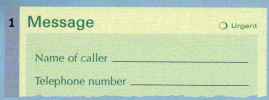

1 **Message**                                    ○ Urgent

    Name of caller _____
    Telephone number _____

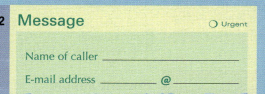

2 **Message**                                    ○ Urgent

    Name of caller _____
    E-mail address _____ @ _____

**B** Listen again to the beginning of the first conversation and complete it.

| You hear: | You say: |
|---|---|
| *Hello. Mr Bashir's _____ _____ .* | *Hello. Can I _____ to Mr Bashir, please?* |
| *Who's calling?* | *This is _____ _____ in _____ _____ .* |
| *I'm _____ , but Mr Bashir _____ here today.* | *Can he _____ me tomorrow, please?* |

Your **turn**

**C** Work in pairs. Student A looks at this page. Student B looks at page 152.

**Student A**
You are Saleem Bashir's personal assistant. He is not in the office today. Write down the details of the person who calls.
*How do you spell your name, please?*

Name _____
Telephone number _____
E-mail address _____

## Checklist

✔ present simple: *live, love, work …*
✔ workplaces: *factory, company restaurant …*
✔ phone someone and leave a message: *Can he call me tomorrow, please?*
✔ spell names and e-mail addresses

# 5 She goes to Spain

## Reading

**A** **Read the text.**

I'm Astrid Schmidt, a director at Supersport in Frankfurt. I like my work, but I like holidays too!
I take my summer holiday in July: I go to Spain or Italy for three weeks. It's important to have a long break.
In the winter, I go skiing in the Alps. I go for a week in February or March.
At weekends, I go to my house in the country. It's important to relax at weekends too.

⚠ About five million Germans and five million British people go on holiday to Spain every year. More than 50 million people go there altogether.

**B** **Now write *T* (true) or *F* (false).**

1 Astrid likes holidays. __T__

2 She takes her summer holiday in August. _____

3 She goes to Spain or Italy in the summer. _____

4 She goes skiing in January. _____

5 At weekends she goes to her house in the country. _____

6 She thinks it's important to relax at weekends. _____

## Grammar

### Present simple

You can use the present simple to talk about routines.
*She always goes to Spain in July.*

You ask questions with *Does* and the base form of the verb. You make negatives with *doesn't* and the base form of the verb.
*Does she take a break in August? – No, she doesn't.*

**A** **Complete the tables.**

| | he | take a break in August? | No, he _____ . |
|---|---|---|---|
| _Does_ | she | go to Spain or Italy? | Yes, she _____ . |
| | it | leave at 10.15? | No, _____ _____ . |

| He | | take a break in August. He takes a break in July. |
|---|---|---|
| She | doesn't | _go_ to France. She _____ to Spain or Italy. |
| It | | _____ at 10.15. It leaves at 11.15. |

**B** 🔘 **5.1 Now listen, check and repeat.**

**C** **Work in pairs. Ask and answer questions about Astrid Schmidt.**

1 holiday / July
**A:** *Does she go on holiday in July?* **B:** *Yes, she does.*

2 Portugal / August

3 go skiing / winter

4 go skiing / the Pyrenees

5 stay / Frankfurt / weekends

■ More information: Grammar overview page 105

## Vocabulary and speaking

**Ⓐ Look at these expressions.**

| Times of the day and week |
| --- |
| ▪ **in the** morning/afternoon |
| ▪ **at** night |
| ▪ **at** weekends |
| ▪ **at the** weekend |

| Times of the year |
| --- |
| ▪ **in** January, February, March, April, May, June, July, August, September, October, November, December |
| ▪ **in the** spring, summer, autumn, winter |

**Your turn Ⓑ Work in pairs. Talk about:**

- when you go on holiday   *I usually go on holiday in June.*
- where you go on holiday   *I usually go to Greece.*

**Ⓒ Now talk about your partner.**

*… usually goes to Greece in June.*

## Listening

**Ⓐ 5.2 Listen and complete.**

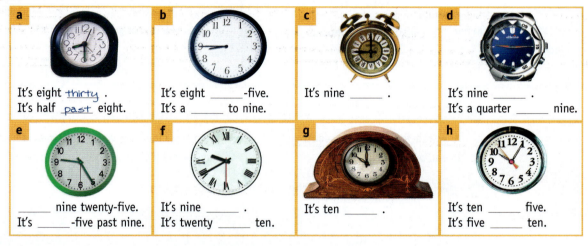

| **a** | **b** | **c** | **d** |
| --- | --- | --- | --- |
| It's eight <u>thirty</u> .<br>It's half <u>past</u> eight. | It's eight _____-five.<br>It's a _____ to nine. | It's nine _____ . | It's nine _____ .<br>It's a quarter _____ nine. |

| **e** | **f** | **g** | **h** |
| --- | --- | --- | --- |
| _____ nine twenty-five.<br>It's _____-five past nine. | It's nine _____ .<br>It's twenty _____ ten. | It's ten _____ . | It's ten _____ five.<br>It's five _____ ten. |

**Ⓑ Now say the times.**

## ⓞN THE LINE

**Ⓐ 5.3 Astrid and an Australian friend, Julia, decide to go skiing in Innsbruck. Listen to the three conversations and complete the table.**

| | What time is it? | Where is Astrid? | Where is Julia? |
| --- | --- | --- | --- |
| **1** | 9.15 am | At the check-in desk at the airport | At the hotel entrance |
| **2** | | | |
| **3** | | | |

**Your turn Ⓑ You travel to another city and you phone an old friend, Anna. Tell her where you are.**

A: *Hello, Anna. It's …*
B: *Hello, …*
A: *Where are you?*
B: *I'm …*
A: *OK, see you soon!*

| **at** | the airport/train station/<br>bus station<br>a hotel/café |
| --- | --- |
| **in** | a taxi/car |
| **on** | a bus/train/plane |

## Checklist

✓ use the present simple to talk about routines: *I take my holiday in July.*

✓ prepositions of time: *at night, in April, in the summer …*

✓ prepositions of place: *I'm in a taxi at the airport.*

✓ say times: *It's five past ten.*

15

# 6 How do you relax?

## Reading

**A** Read the e-mails.

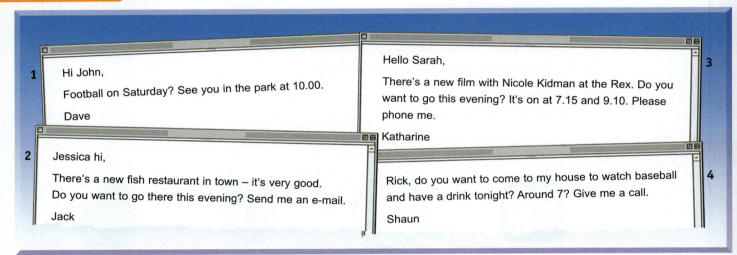

**1** Hi John,

Football on Saturday? See you in the park at 10.00.

Dave

**2** Jessica hi,

There's a new fish restaurant in town – it's very good. Do you want to go there this evening? Send me an e-mail.

Jack

**3** Hello Sarah,

There's a new film with Nicole Kidman at the Rex. Do you want to go this evening? It's on at 7.15 and 9.10. Please phone me.

Katharine

**4** Rick, do you want to come to my house to watch baseball and have a drink tonight? Around 7? Give me a call.

Shaun

**B** What activities are in the e-mails in exercise A? Circle the correct answer for each e-mail.

**1** watch football / play football
**2** eat out / eat in
**3** go to the cinema / watch a film on television
**4** play baseball / watch baseball on television

## Listening and speaking

**A** Listen and complete the market researcher's form.

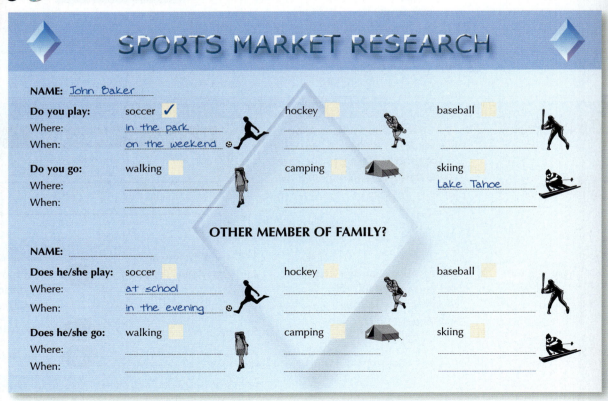

### SPORTS MARKET RESEARCH

**NAME:** John Baker

| **Do you play:** | soccer ✔ | hockey ☐ | baseball ☐ |
| Where: | in the park | | |
| When: | on the weekend | | |

| **Do you go:** | walking ☐ | camping ☐ | skiing ☐ |
| Where: | | | Lake Tahoe |
| When: | | | |

### OTHER MEMBER OF FAMILY?

**NAME:**

| **Does he/she play:** | soccer ☐ | hockey ☐ | baseball ☐ |
| Where: | at school | | |
| When: | in the evening | | |

| **Does he/she go:** | walking ☐ | camping ☐ | skiing ☐ |
| Where: | | | |
| When: | | | |

**B** Work in pairs. Student A is the interviewer; Student B is John Baker. Ask and answer the questions from the form in exercise A.

(Student B: You are American, so you say *On the weekend*, not *At the weekend*!)

**Grammar** question words

*When do you play football?*

**A** 6.2 **Listen and complete.**

1 <u>How</u> do you relax?
2 When do you _____ football?
3 _____ do you play?
4 Who do you play _____ ?
5 _____ often do you win?
6 Why do you _____ football and not hockey?

**B** **Now match questions 1–6 above to the answers below.**

a [2] At the weekend.
b [ ] I play football.
c [ ] With friends.
d [ ] Not every time!
e [ ] Because it's more exciting!
f [ ] In the park.

**C** 6.3 **Now listen and check.**

Your turn **D** **Work in pairs. Ask and answer questions about your free time.**

▶ More practice:
Workbook page 12

A: *How do you relax?*
B: *I go to the cinema.*

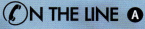 N THE LINE **A** 6.4 **Listen to the phone call to Magic World Park and complete the information.**

# Magic World Park summer programme

| Park | opens: | closes: |
|---|---|---|
| | <u>10.00 am</u> | <u>9.00 pm</u> |
| **Restaurant** | opens: | last meal: |
| | _____ | _____ |
| **Ghost train** | first train leaves: | last train leaves: |
| | _____ | _____ |
| **Cinema** | first film show starts: | last film show starts: |
| | _____ | _____ |

Your turn **B** **Work in pairs. Student A looks at this page. Student B looks at page 152.**

**Student A**
Phone Student B to get times for the winter programme.
*What time does the park open?*
*When's the first film show?*

**Writing** **A** **Look at the e-mails on page 16. Write an e-mail to a friend about something to do this evening or this weekend.**

**Checklist**
✓ *do(es)* with question words: Where does your son play football?
✓ free time expressions: *have a drink, watch a film*
✓ ask and answer about times: When does the train leave? – At 10.30 am.

17

# Review 1–6

**A  Match the questions to the answers.**

1  What's your name?

2  Where are you from?

3  Where's Krakow?

4  What's your job?

5  And your friend – what's her name?

6  And what's her job?

7  Where's she from?

a  I'm from Krakow.

b  She's an engineer.

c  I'm an accountant.

d  It's in Poland.

e  My name's Susannah.

f  She's from Warsaw.

g  Her name's Wanda.

**B  Circle the correct response.**

1  Hello, I'm Harry Esposito.
   a  Yes.          **b**  Hello, I'm ... Nice to meet you.      c  Thanks.

2  Here's my card.
   a  Thank you.      b  Yes, I do.                              c  Yes, it is.

3  Where are you from?
   a  Are you?        b  No.                                    c  I'm from ...

4  Goodbye.
   a  Hi.            b  Bye.                                     c  Hello.

**C  Correct the sentences. There is one mistake in each sentence.**

1  How many employees ~~is~~ *are* there in your company?

2  In this building there is 50 offices.

3  A accountant works in this office.

4  There am a special office for the designers.

5  There aren't a company restaurant.

6  There are a car park for 200 cars.

**D  Complete the crossword about jobs and workplaces.**

**Across**

2  a place where you can see the things a company sells (8)

3  someone who designs things (8)

6  someone who manages people (7)

9  a place where they make things (7)

10  a shop (5)

**Down**

1  someone who answers the phone and writes letters (9)

4  someone who designs machines (8)

5  someone who works with money and numbers (10)

7  someone who works for a company (8)

8  a place where people do business (6)

18

**E** 🔊 **R1.1** **Listen to the announcements and complete the flight information.**

| DEPARTURES | TO | GATE |
|---|---|---|
| 1 RG 993 | RIO | 44 |
| 2 | ROME | |
| 3 | | 9 |
| 4 | | |
| 5 | | |
| 6 | | |

**F** **Read about these four people.**

> Anita, Ben, Chris and Delia each live in a different city in Canada: Halifax, Montreal, Toronto and Vancouver.
>
> They each work for a different company: Walters, Xenon, Youngs and Zetters.
>
> Anita lives in Montreal and works at Xenon.
> Ben lives in Halifax and doesn't work at Youngs or Zetters.
> Chris doesn't live in Vancouver and doesn't work at Youngs.
> Delia doesn't live in Toronto and doesn't work at Walters or Zetters.

**G** **Work in pairs. Ask and answer questions about where Anita, Ben, Chris and Delia live and work.**

**A:** *Does Anita live in Montreal?*
**B:** *Yes, she does.*

**H** **Now complete the table in pairs, giving your reasons.**

*Anita lives in Montreal and Ben lives in Halifax. We know that Chris doesn't live in Vancouver, so he lives in Toronto.*

| | lives in | works at |
|---|---|---|
| Anita | Montreal | Xenon |
| Ben | | |
| Chris | | |
| Delia | | |

**I** **Put the sentences in order to make a telephone conversation.**

a ☐ *Goodbye.*
b ☐ *Hello.* (1)
c ☐ *I'm sorry, but she isn't here today.*
d ☐ *OK. I'll ask her to call you.*
e ☐ *What's your number?*
f ☐ *Who's calling?*
g ☐ *Bye.*
h ☐ *Oh. Can she call me tomorrow, please?*
i ☐ *Hello. Can I speak to Fiona, please?*
j ☐ *It's 00 32 2 982 2631.*
k ☐ *Thank you.*
l ☐ *This is Monique Colbert in Brussels.*

**J** **You have a new job in another company. Write an e-mail to a friend about:**

- where you work.
- what time you start and finish work.
- your office: is it nice?
- the furniture: is it modern?
- what you do at lunchtime.

MODULE

2

SPLASH POOLS

Sven Karlsson works for Splash Pools, a company that sells pools and saunas. Energy Gyms places a big order, but the saunas are delivered late and the customer wants to know why.

Do you go to a lot of meetings? Who with?

Give directions to places in your town.

Is the customer always right?

Give examples of typical phone messages that you take at home/work.

What date is it today? When's your birthday?

What are the other people in your company/school doing now? Do they do these things every day?

 Review 7–12

# 7 We get a lot of visitors

## Reading

**A** Look at the website and read the article.

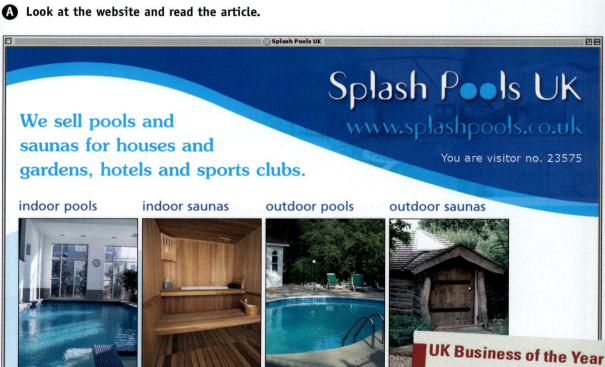

**B** Now match the questions to the answers.

1 How many employees are there in the UK?
2 How many showrooms are there?
3 How many visitors to the website are there?
4 How many employees are there in Europe?
5 Does Sven like his work?

a Three.
b One hundred and twenty.
c Yes, he likes it a lot.
d There are a lot.
e Twenty-five.

## Grammar

**how many; a lot**

You can ask about numbers like this:
*How many employees are there in the UK?*
*How many saunas do you sell?*

You can also use *a lot* as an adverb.
*Do you like your work? – Yes, I like it a lot.*

You can answer like this:
*About twenty. / Not many. / Not a lot. / A lot.*

**A** Complete the questions.

1
A: *How* _many_ *people* _do_ *you work with?*
B: *Not many. There are only three people in my office.*

2
A: _____ _____ *employees are* _____ *in your company?*
B: *There are a lot – more than 900 in different places.*

3
A: *Do you have a* _____ *of customers?*
B: *We don't have many. There are only three or four, but they are very big customers.*

4
A: *How* _____ *hours* _____ _____ *work every week?*
B: *I work a lot – about 65 hours a week.*

5
A: _____ _____ *weeks' holiday* _____ _____ *have every year?*
B: *Not many. Only two.*

**B** Now practise saying the questions and answers in pairs.

**Your turn**

**C** Work in pairs. Student A looks at this page. Student B looks at page 153.

**Student A**

- Phone Student B in the warehouse and ask about the number of products there are.

  A: *How many indoor saunas are there?*

  B: *Not many – only three.*

- Complete the table with the information.

| indoor saunas | *not many – 3* |
|---|---|
| outdoor saunas | |
| small Jacuzzis | |
| large Jacuzzis | |

- More information:
Grammar overview
page 112
- More practice:
Workbook page 16

**Vocabulary and expressions**

**A** Complete the table.

**Days of the week**

Mon _d a y_     Tues _ _ _     Wed _ _ _ _ _ _     Th _ _ _ _ _ _     F _ _ _ _ _

Sat _ _ _ _ _ _ + S _ _ _ _ _ _ = the week _ _ _

🇬🇧 at the weekend/at weekends, 🇺🇸 on the weekend/on weekends

yester _ _ _ ← to _ _ _ → tomor _ _ _

**ON THE LINE** **A** 🔊 7.1 Listen to two people arranging a meeting. Write *T* (true) or *F* (false).

1 Sven Karlsson phones Carole Bruckner. _F_

2 Carole works for Energy Gyms. _____

3 She wants to buy pools. _____

4 Sven doesn't know Energy Gyms. _____

5 Carole wants to visit the Splash Pools showroom. _____

6 They arrange to meet on Friday. _____

7 Sven gives the address of Splash Pools to Carole. _____

**Your turn**

**B** Work in pairs. Student A looks at this page. Student B looks at page 153.

**Student A**

- Phone B and ask for a meeting at B's office. *Can we meet at your office?*
- When B suggests a time, say it isn't possible and suggest another day and time. *That isn't possible. How about ... ?*
- After B agrees, say goodbye.

**Checklist**

✓ how many; a lot: *How many employees are there? – Not many.*

✓ days of the week: *Monday, Tuesday ...*

✓ arrange a meeting: *How about Thursday?*

# 8 Turn left at the lights

**Reading and vocabulary**

**A** Complete the directions on the Splash Pools website, using the words in the box.

| bridge | corner | crossroads | main road | side street | traffic lights | tube station |
|---|---|---|---|---|---|---|

**B** Now mark the position of Splash Pools on the map.

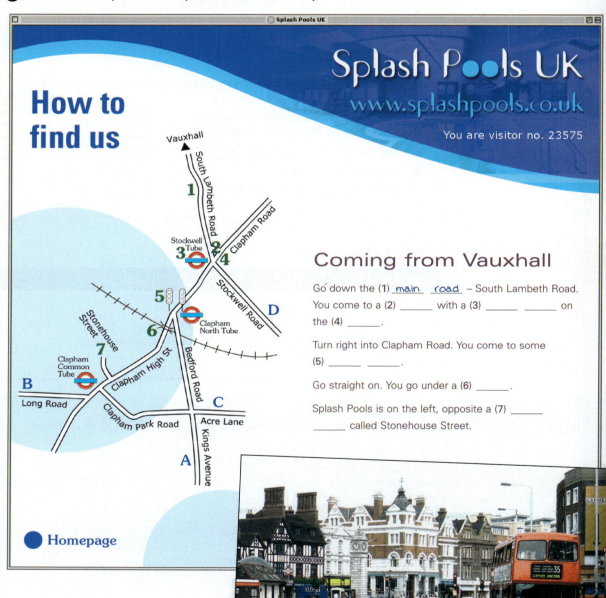

Splash Pools UK
www.splashpools.co.uk
You are visitor no. 23575

**How to find us**

Vauxhall

South Lambeth Road
Clapham Road
Stockwell Tube
Stockwell Road
Stonehouse Street
Clapham North Tube
Clapham Common Tube
Clapham High St
Bedford Road
Long Road
Clapham Park Road
Acre Lane
Kings Avenue

## Coming from Vauxhall

Go down the (1) _main road_ – South Lambeth Road. You come to a (2) _____ with a (3) _____ _____ on the (4) _____.

Turn right into Clapham Road. You come to some (5) _____ _____.

Go straight on. You go under a (6) _____.

Splash Pools is on the left, opposite a (7) _____ _____ called Stonehouse Street.

Homepage

▶ More practice: Workbook page 19

*C*N THE LINE **Ⓐ** 🔘 8.1 **Carole is driving to the Splash Pools showroom. She is lost. Listen to the phone call. At the beginning of the conversation, where is Carole – A, B, C or D?**

Your **turn 1** **Ⓑ** **Work in pairs. Student A looks at this page. Student B looks at page 153.**

**Student A**

You are the receptionist at Splash Pools. Student B phones you three times. Look at the map on page 24 and explain how to find your company.

Your **turn 2** **Ⓒ** **Explain how to get to your office from different places.**

## Listening and speaking

**Ⓐ** 🔘 8.2 **Listen and complete the three conversations.**

**Conversation 1**

A: *Tea?*
B: *Yes, please .*
A: *Sugar?*
B: *Two, _____ .*
A: *Here you are.*
B: _____ .

**Conversation 2**

A: *Would you like a coffee?*
B: *Yes, _____ .*
A: *How do you like it?*
B: *White, one sugar, _____ .*
A: *Here you are.*
B: _____ .

**Conversation 3**

A: *Would you like some juice?*
B: _____ , _____ .
A: *Sure?*
B: *I'm OK, _____ .*

**Ⓑ** 🔘 8.3 **Carole Bruckner is visiting Sven Karlsson at the Splash Pools showroom. Listen to the conversation. Write *T* (true) or *F* (false).**

1 Carole arrives at Splash Pools and Sven comes to meet her. ___T___
2 Carole does not say why she is late and does not say sorry. _____
3 Sven offers Carole something to drink and she asks for tea. _____
4 Carole says that her company now has seven gyms. _____
5 Carole says that next year her company wants to open twelve more gyms. _____

⊙ On a typical day in Europe there are 17 million meetings.

Your **turn** **Ⓒ** **Work in pairs. Offer things, using *Would you ... ?* Accept or refuse, using *Yes, please, Thanks* and *No, thanks*.**

## Speaking

**Ⓐ** **Work in pairs. Student A looks at this page. Student B looks at page 153.**

**Student A**

You are Sven Karlsson.
• Ask a new customer (Student B) about what they need. *How many indoor saunas do you need? When do you need them?*
• Complete the table with the information.

|  | number | delivery |
|---|---|---|
| indoor saunas | 30 | next month |
| outdoor saunas |  |  |
| small Jacuzzis |  |  |
| large Jacuzzis |  |  |

Checklist ✓names of places: *station, crossroads ...* ✓ask for and give directions: *Where's the showroom?* – *It's opposite Stonehouse Street.* ✓make offers, and accept or refuse them: *Would you like a coffee?* – *Yes, please. / No, thanks.*

# 9 Can I help you?

## Vocabulary

**A** Match the words to their meanings.

| | | | |
|---|---|---|---|
| 1 | customer | **a** | how much you pay for something |
| 2 | supplier | **b** | something that you buy |
| 3 | product | **c** | less than the normal price for something |
| 4 | price | **d** | someone who buys something |
| 5 | discount | **e** | someone who sells something |
| 6 | order | **f** | when a supplier sends products to a customer |
| 7 | delivery | **g** | the products supplied to a customer |

● More information:
Vocabulary builder
page 101

**B** The salespeople at one company (not at Splash Pools!) have these rules in their office. What do you think about them? Use some of the answers in the box and give your reasons.

> I agree.   I disagree.   It depends.   That's right.   That's wrong.

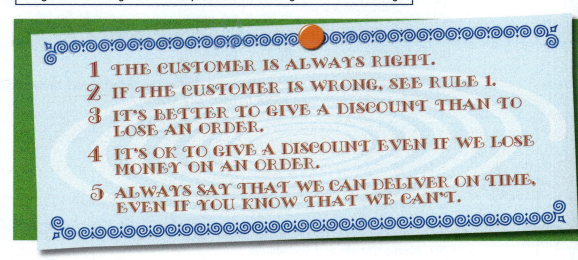

1 THE CUSTOMER IS ALWAYS RIGHT.
2 IF THE CUSTOMER IS WRONG, SEE RULE 1.
3 IT'S BETTER TO GIVE A DISCOUNT THAN TO LOSE AN ORDER.
4 IT'S OK TO GIVE A DISCOUNT EVEN IF WE LOSE MONEY ON AN ORDER.
5 ALWAYS SAY THAT WE CAN DELIVER ON TIME, EVEN IF YOU KNOW THAT WE CAN'T.

## Grammar

### *can* and *can't*

*We **can** deliver ten next month.*

**A** Match the uses of *can* and *can't* to the sentences.

1 [ c ] *can*: talk/ask about possibilities
2 [  ] *can*: make offers
3 [  ] *can*: ask for things
4 [  ] *can't*: talk about things you are not able to do
5 [  ] *can't*: talk about things you are not allowed to do

**a** We can't deliver before next year.
**b** You can't smoke in here.
**c** When can you deliver?
**d** Can you send a brochure?
**e** Can I help you?

**B** 🔘 9.1 Now listen and repeat.

**C** Match the questions to the answers.

1 Can I have two cups of coffee – one black, one white?
2 Can you give me your name?
3 Can we have a discount of 15 per cent?
4 Can I take those bags for you?
5 When can we have the products?
6 You can use the gym between 7 am and 6 pm.

**a** Pym. P-Y-M.
**b** One black, one white – no problem.
**c** Isn't it open in the evenings?
**d** I'm sorry, we can only give 12 per cent.
**e** It's OK, thanks – they aren't heavy.
**f** Next month.

● More information:
Grammar overview
page 109

► More practice:
Workbook page 20

**D** Now practise saying the complete exchanges in pairs.

## ON THE LINE

**A** 9.2 Carole Bruckner phones Sven Karlsson to place an order. Listen and write down the details of her order.

| product: | indoor saunas |
| --- | --- |
| number: | 20 |
| colours: | blue, white |
| delivery: | _____ next month<br>_____ the month after |
| price: | _____ |
| normal discount: | _____ |
| discount for this customer: | _____ |

Your **turn**

**B** Work in pairs. Student A looks at this page. Student B looks at page 154.

**Student A**

You are Sven Karlsson. An old customer (Student B) phones you to place a new order for Jacuzzis.
*Hello. Sven Karlsson speaking. Can I help you?*
Write down the details of their order.

| product: | indoor Jacuzzis |
| --- | --- |
| number: | _____ |
| colours: | _____ _____ _____ |
| delivery: | next month |
| price: | £6,000 |
| normal discount: | 10% |
| discount for this customer: | 12% |

## Writing

**A** You are the customer from Your turn exercise B. Complete the e-mail to Sven Karlsson.

Dear Sven,

Following our phone conversation, we want to place an order for [1]indoor

_____ : 5 [2]_____ and 5 [3]_____ . The basic price is [4]_____ , with a discount

of [5]_____ . (Thanks, Sven!) Delivery is [6]_____ _____ .

Best wishes,

_____

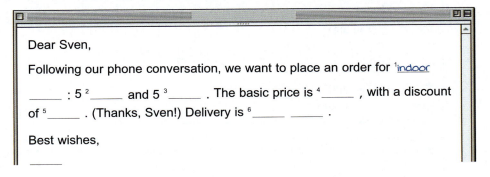

**Checklist**
✓ **can:** *Can I have a coffee? We can deliver on time.*
✓ **can't:** *You can't smoke in here.*
✓ **talk about products, prices, orders and delivery:** *We can give a discount of 12 per cent.*

# 10 I'm buying a house

## Reading  Ⓐ Read the e-mail.

From: teresa.pym@whamm.com
To: info@splashpools.co.uk
Date: 20 October 200-
Subject: Jacuzzis

I am writing to ask for your help. I am buying a house in south London. We are planning the garden now, and we are looking for an outdoor Jacuzzi. My children and I are hoping to move into the house very soon – this week. Please can you tell me about the Jacuzzis that you sell?

Best wishes,
Teresa Pym

Ⓑ Now write *T* (true) or *F* (false).

1 Teresa Pym is writing to ask about pools. _F_
2 She is buying a house. _____
3 She and her family are planning the garden. _____
4 She is looking for an outdoor Jacuzzi. _____
5 She is hoping to move into the house next year. _____

## Grammar  present continuous

*We're planning the garden now.*
You can use the present continuous to talk about things happening now.
You make the present continuous with *am/are/is* and the *-ing* form of the verb.

Ⓐ Complete the tables.

| | |
|---|---|
| I'm___ (I am) | |
| You're___ (You are) | |
| He's___/She___ (He/She is) | planning the garden now. |
| We___ (We are) | |
| You___ (You are) | |
| They___ (They are) | |

| | |
|---|---|
| Is she looking___ for a sauna? | No, she isn't looking for a sauna. She's ___ for a Jacuzzi. |
| Are you hop___ to buy it soon? | Yes, we ___ . We're ___ to buy it this week. |
| Are they mov___ into the house today? | No, they ___ . |

■ More information: Grammar overview page 106

▶ More practice: Workbook page 22

Ⓑ  Now listen, check and repeat.

**Listening and speaking**

**A**  **10.2** Sven is talking to Tania, a sales rep at Splash Pools. Listen to the conversation and match the sales reps to what they are doing.

| | | | |
|---|---|---|---|
| **1** Tania | | **a** | He's visiting a customer. |
| **2** Len | | **b** | She's working on a big order for Brilliant Gyms. |
| **3** Cathy | | **c** | He's swimming in the Mediterranean. |
| **4** Brian | | **d** | She's making coffee. |

Your **turn**

**B** Work in pairs. Student A looks at this page. Student B looks at page 154.

**Student A**

It's one week later. You are Sven Karlsson. You are talking to Tania again.

• Tell Tania (Student B) you are looking for someone to work on a new order from the Supreme Sports Club (SSC). *I'm looking for someone to work on a new order from the SSC.*

• Ask Tania what she is doing.

• Ask Tania what Len, Cathy and Brian are doing.

• When Tania asks, tell her how much SSC are spending – one million pounds.

• When Tania offers to work on this order, accept and thank her.

• End the conversation.

**(!) When you phone someone in a company, there is only a 1-in-3 chance that you talk to the person you want.**

**ON THE LINE**

**A** 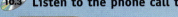 **10.3** Listen to the phone call to Splash Pools and <u>underline</u> the expressions you hear.

| **Receptionist** | **Caller** |
|---|---|
| *Who's calling, please?* | *Is that … ?* |
| *Unfortunately he's/she's …* | *I'm phoning about …* |
| *Can I take a message?* | *Can you give him/her a message?* |
| *Can I ask him/her to call you back?* | *Can you ask him/her to call me back?* |
| *Does he/she have your number?* | |

Your **turn**

**B** The Splash Pools receptionist takes a message from a caller, Jessica Fonesca. Work in pairs. Student A is the receptionist and Student B is Jessica Fonesca. Have a similar conversation to the one you heard, using some of the expressions in exercise A.

**A:** *Hello. Is that Splash Pools?*

**B:** *Yes – who's calling, please?*

| | |
|---|---|
| **Message for:** | Sven Karlsson |
| **Caller's name:** | Jessica Fonesca |
| **Company:** | Splash Pools, New York office |
| **Called at:** | 10.20 am **on:** 21st October |
| **Message:** | She is in UK at the moment. She wants to see you. |
| **Call back?** | On Monday morning before 10 am at her hotel – Ritz, Piccadilly |
| **Number:** | 020 7493 8181 |

**Checklist** ✔ present continuous: *She's making coffee.*    ✔ leave and take a message on the phone: *Can you give him a message? I can't make it.*

# 11 What's Sven doing?

## Reading

**A** Read the e-mail.

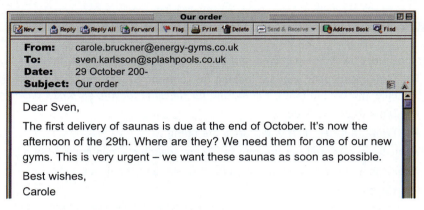

> **Our order**
>
> New ▾ | Reply | Reply All | Forward | Flag | Print | Delete | Send & Receive ▾ | Address Book | Find
>
> **From:** carole.bruckner@energy-gyms.co.uk
> **To:** sven.karlsson@splashpools.co.uk
> **Date:** 29 October 200-
> **Subject:** Our order
>
> Dear Sven,
>
> The first delivery of saunas is due at the end of October. It's now the afternoon of the 29th. Where are they? We need them for one of our new gyms. This is very urgent – we want these saunas as soon as possible.
>
> Best wishes,
> Carole

**B** Now answer the questions.

1 Who is the e-mail from?
2 What is the date?
3 Who is it to?
4 What is it about?
5 What does Carole want?

## ON THE LINE

**A** 11.1 Listen to the conversation between Sven and his assistant, Tracey. Write *T* (true) or *F* (false).

1 Sven phones Tracey. _F_
2 Sven is playing golf. _____
3 He's losing. _____
4 Tracey tells Sven about the e-mail from Carole Bruckner. _____
5 Sven tells Tracey to phone Carole. _____

**Your turn**

**B** Work in pairs. Student A looks at this page. Student B looks at page 155.

**Student A**

You are Tracey, Sven's assistant. You call Carole Bruckner (Student B).

- Thank her for her e-mail.   *Thank you for your e-mail.*
- Tell her Sven is out of the office, visiting another customer.
- He is checking with the warehouse about her sauna delivery.
- She can phone Sven on Monday morning – ask her if she has the number.
- When Carole replies, tell her that Sven has her number.
- End the conversation.

## Grammar

**present continuous with question words**

*What are you doing?*

**A** Complete the table, using the question words in the box.

| How | ~~What~~ | When |
| --- | --- | --- |
| Where | Who | Why |

| | |
| --- | --- |
| _What_ 's (What is) Sven doing? | He's playing golf. |
| _____'s he playing? | At a golf club near London. |
| _____'s he playing? | On Friday afternoon. |
| _____'s he playing? | A customer. |
| _____'s he playing? | He wants an order. |
| _____'s he playing? | Very well. He's winning. |

▶ More practice: Workbook page 24

**B** 11.2 Now listen, check and repeat.

## Speaking

**A** Work in pairs. Student A looks at this page. Student B looks at page 155.

**Student A**

You play three visitors who have appointments to see Sven Karlsson. (Student B is Sven's assistant, Tracey.)

**1** Arabella Adams, Monday 1st November, 11 am

**2** Bob Brandt, Tuesday 2nd November, 1.45 pm

**3** Carla Cobb, Wednesday 3rd November, 3.10 pm

- Start the conversations like this:

 **A:** *My name's Arabella Adams. Can I see Sven Karlsson, please? I have an appointment with him.*

 **B:** *Are you sure?*

 **A:** *Yes, it's in my diary. Monday the first of November, 11 o'clock.*

 **B:** *I'm sorry, Ms Adams. He's visiting a new customer.*

 **A:** *I see.*

- When Tracey gives the time for another appointment, accept it.

 *Tuesday the ninth of November at 4 o'clock. OK.*

- Then say goodbye.

## Vocabulary

**A** Complete the table.

| Dates | Say ... | Write ... |
|---|---|---|
| 1st  first | the first of May or  <u>May   the   first</u> | 1st May or May 1st |
| 2nd  second | the second of May or  _____  _____  _____ | 2nd May or  _____  _____ |
| 3rd  third | the third of May or  _____  _____  _____ | _____  _____  or  _____  _____ |
| 4th  fourth | the fourth of May or  _____  _____  _____ | _____  _____  or  _____  _____ |
| 5th  fifth | the  _____  of May or  _____  _____  _____ | _____  _____  or  _____  _____ |

In the US, you can also say *May first, May second,* etc.

You also use these numbers to talk about **streets** in a city, especially in the US (*the corner of Sixth Avenue and 42nd Street*) and **floors** in a building (*second floor, third floor* ...).

**B** 🔘 Now listen, check and repeat.

**C** Say these dates for holidays.

January 1st   New Year's Day          December 25th   Christmas Day

**D** Say these street names.

3rd Avenue
5th Avenue

10th Avenue
42nd Street
119th Street

- More information: Vocabulary builder page 103

 **E** When are the important holidays in your country?

**Your turn 2** **F** Work in pairs. Ask and answer questions.

 **A:** *When's your birthday?*

 **B:** *It's on ...*

## Checklist

✓ present continuous with question words: *What are you doing?*

✓ dates, floors and streets: *1st, 2nd, 3rd* ...

# 12 The truck's leaving now

**Reading** | Ⓐ Read the webpage.

**Splash Pools UK**

Swedish saunas & pools

● Homepage

## How we deliver your order

Swedesaunas <u>make</u> saunas at their factory in Kalmar, Sweden. They deliver to customers all over the world. Splash Pools are one of their customers in the UK.

Swedesaunas get an order from Splash Pools for some saunas. They put the saunas on a truck. The truck goes to Gothenburg and drives onto the ferry. The ferry leaves in the evening. It crosses the North Sea and arrives in Harwich the next day. The truck drives off the ferry.

The truck goes to the Swedesaunas warehouse near London. From the warehouse, another truck delivers the saunas to the Splash Pools showroom in south London, or directly to Splash Pools' customers.

The delivery usually takes two to three days.

**Vocabulary** | Ⓐ Match the words to their meanings.

1 ferry — **a** when products are taken to a customer
2 distribution — **b** a building for products before they are delivered
3 truck — **c** a ship for cars and trucks
4 warehouse — **d** a vehicle for moving products by road

Ⓑ Now write *T* (true) or *F* (false).

1 Swedesaunas make saunas in Stockholm. ___F___
2 The saunas go from Sweden to the UK by truck and ferry. _____
3 The ferry takes 48 hours to cross the North Sea. _____
4 The ferry arrives in Harwich. _____
5 The Swedesaunas warehouse is near London. _____
6 The saunas always go directly to Splash Pools' customers. _____

Ⓒ Now <u>underline</u> all the verbs in the present simple on the webpage.

⚠ Rotterdam is the biggest port in the world. Over 300 million tonnes of products go through it every year.

## Grammar present simple and present continuous

You can use the present simple to talk about routines.

*The ferry cross**es** the North Sea and arriv**es** in Harwich the next day.*

You use the present continuous to say what is happening now.

*It's midnight. The ferry **is** cross**ing** the North Sea.*
*It's 7 am. The ferry **is** arriv**ing** in Harwich.*

But you do not use some verbs in the present continuous: *like, know, need, understand, want.*

*I <u>know</u> Sven Karlsson. not ~~I am knowing Sven Karlsson.~~*

▶ More practice:
Workbook page 26

## ☏N THE LINE  Ⓐ

🔘 12.1 **Carole Bruckner of Energy Gyms is waiting for delivery of her saunas. On Monday, she phones Sven Karlsson to ask where they are. Listen to the conversation and <u>underline</u> the expressions you hear.**

**Complaining**
*I'm calling to complain about …*

**Apologies**
*(Please accept) our apologies for the delay/inconvenience. (formal)*
*We're (very) sorry about …*
*We're doing everything we can to solve the problem.*

**Accepting apologies**
*I accept your apologies. (formal)*
*That's all right. (less formal)*
*No problem. (less formal)*

Your turn  Ⓑ **Work in pairs. Student A looks at this page. Student B looks at page 156.**

**Student A**

You are Carole Bruckner. It is Tuesday, 2nd November.

- Phone Sven Karlsson (Student B) at Splash Pools to find out where your saunas are.
  *Hello, Sven. I'm still worried about the delivery. Where are my saunas now?*
- Accept Sven's apologies and end the conversation.
- It is now Thursday. You are still waiting for the saunas. Phone Sven again.

## Writing  Ⓐ **You are Sven Karlsson. It is Thursday 4th November. Write an e-mail to Carole Bruckner:**

- to say that you are delivering the saunas today. *This is to confirm that …*
- to apologise for the late delivery.

## Checklist

✓ distribution and delivery: *ferry, warehouse …*

✓ the difference between the present simple and the present continuous

✓ confirm: *This is to confirm that …*

✓ complain: *I'm phoning to complain about late delivery.*

✓ apologise and accept apologies: *I'm sorry about this problem. – That's all right.*

# Review 7–12

**Ⓐ Look at these questions about a town called Dayton. Circle the answer that is correct in normal spoken English.**

**1** How many people live there?
  ⓐ A lot: about 10,000.
  **b** Many: about 10,000.

**2** Does Dayton have a lot of banks?
  **a** No, it doesn't have no banks.
  **b** No, it doesn't have many banks.

**3** Are there many shops?
  **a** Yes, there are a lot.
  **b** Yes, many.

**4** How many schools are there?
  **a** A lot: five or six.
  **b** Many: five or six.

**5** Are there many companies?
  **a** Yes, there are a lot of companies.
  **b** Yes, there are many companies.

**6** Do you enjoy living there?
  **a** Yes, I enjoy it very.
  **b** Yes, I enjoy it a lot.

**Ⓑ Correct the sentences, using the present continuous.**

**1** Agneta ⁱˢ/working in her office.

**2** Bob is play golf.

**3** Consuelo are sit in the sauna.

**4** Daniel and Ella is talking to customers in the showroom.

**5** Fabrizio am swim in the pool.

**6** Georgina look at new products.

**7** Harold and Laura wait for a delivery.

**Ⓒ Now change the sentences into questions.**

*Is Agneta working in her office?*

**Ⓓ Complete the text with the present simple or present continuous forms of the verbs in brackets.**

Sigma is a company that ¹_makes_ (make) computers. It ²_____ (have) 3,000 employees. They ³_____ (work) in a factory in Cardiff. They ⁴_____ (make) computers only when they ⁵_____ (get) orders. Trucks ⁶_____ (take) the computers direct to the customers.

This week Sigma ⁷_____ _____ (get) a lot of orders. It's 1.30 pm on Wednesday. The salespeople ⁸_____ _____ (talk) to customers on the phone. The factory employees ⁹_____ _____ (work) on the orders. Office employees ¹⁰_____ _____ (have) lunch in the company restaurant. Trucks ¹¹_____ _____ (leave) Cardiff with computers for a lot of cities in the UK. The director of Sigma is very happy.

**Ⓔ Put the conversations in order. Then practise saying them in pairs.**

**1**
**a** ☐ Here you are.
**b** ☐1 Tea?
**c** ☐ Yes, please.
**d** ☐ Sugar?
**e** ☐ Thank you.
**f** ☐ No, thanks – I don't take sugar.

**2**
**a** ☐ Black, two sugars, please.
**b** ☐ Here you are.
**c** ☐ Thank you.
**d** ☐ Yes, please.
**e** ☐ Would you like a coffee?
**f** ☐ How do you like it?

**3**
**a** ☐ Orange juice or apple juice?
**b** ☐ Would you like some juice?
**c** ☐ Yes, please.
**d** ☐ Apple juice, please.
**e** ☐ Thanks.
**f** ☐ Here you are.

**F** **Work in pairs. Look at the map. Student A is in Lincoln Square in an American city. Ask Student B for directions to:**

- the New England Bus Station.  *Can you tell me the way to the New England Bus Station?*
- the Central Train Station.
- the Mississippi Bookstore.
- the Power Gym Club.
- the Arts Movie Theater.

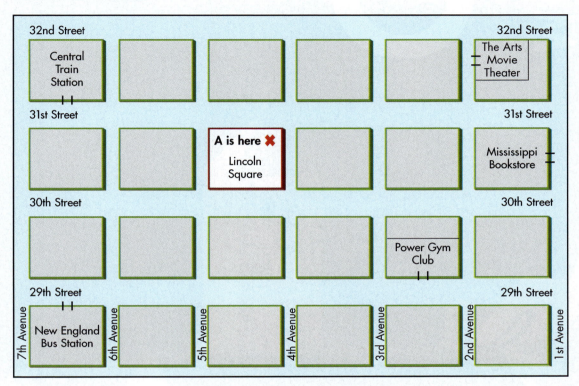

**B uses expressions like these:**

You go down ...   *You go down 31st Street.*
Turn left/right at ...
Turn left/right into ...
Go straight on.
The ... is on the left/right.

**G** **Complete the crossword.**

**Across**
2 What ... do you want – white or blue? (6)
3 If the usual price is €100 and you pay €90, you get a ... (8)
5 someone who buys something (8)
7 something that you buy (7)
9 Can you arrange for ... of the products next week? (8)
10 the money that you pay for something (5)

**Down**
1 a place for products before delivery (9)
4 someone who sells products (8)
6 We want to place an ... for ten saunas. (5)
8 We deliver our products by ... (5)

MODULE

3

MACPHERSON DESIGNS

Fiona Macpherson is a Scottish designer who lives and works in France. Her brother's family come to stay, but she still has a lot of work to finish.

## 13 I work from home

| | |
|---|---|
| Grammar | adverbs *always, usually, often, sometimes, never* |
| Vocabulary | expressions with *work* and *home* |
| On the line | booking a trip |

> Do you usually book trips on the Internet or at a travel agent?

## 14 We're arriving on Monday

| | |
|---|---|
| Grammar | present continuous for future plans; irregular plurals |
| On the line | making a hotel reservation |

> What are you doing tomorrow?

## 15 Can we order, please?

| | |
|---|---|
| Grammar | *was/were* |
| Vocabulary | travel adjectives |
| On the line | talking about a trip |

> Think of some typical restaurant expressions.

## 16 I decided to move to France

| | |
|---|---|
| Grammar | past simple |
| Vocabulary | homeworking |
| Writing | a report about homeworking |

> Do you prefer living in the town or the country?

## 17 Did you get my message?

| | |
|---|---|
| Vocabulary | deadlines |
| On the line | dealing with messages about an urgent job |
| Writing | a business letter |

> What other things can follow 'Did you get my … ?'

## 18 Where did you go?

| | |
|---|---|
| Grammar | past simple with question words |
| On the line | checking information |
| Writing | an e-mail to confirm information |

> Where did you go on your last trip?

 Review 13–18

# 13 I work from home

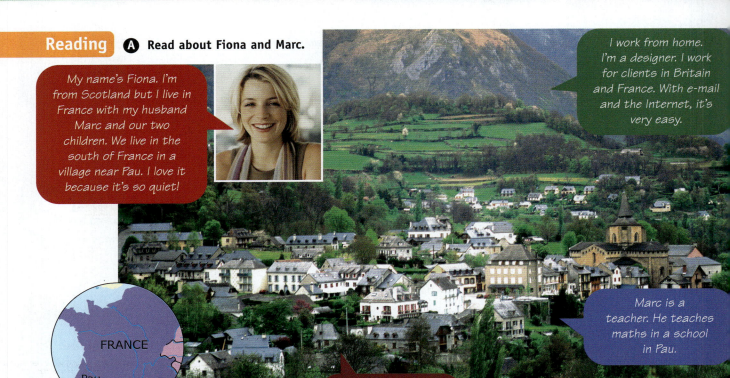

## Reading

**A** Read about Fiona and Marc.

My name's Fiona. I'm from Scotland but I live in France with my husband Marc and our two children. We live in the south of France in a village near Pau. I love it because it's so quiet!

I work from home. I'm a designer. I work for clients in Britain and France. With e-mail and the Internet, it's very easy.

Marc is a teacher. He teaches maths in a school in Pau.

Our children go to school in our village.

FRANCE

Pau

**B** Now answer the questions.

1 Where does Fiona come from?  *She comes from Scotland.*

2 Where does Fiona live?

3 Why does she like it?

4 What does Fiona do?

5 What does Marc do?

6 Where do their children go to school?

## Expressions

**A** Complete the sentences with the correct forms of the expressions in the box.

⚠ In the US, 20 per cent of people work from home, and in Britain 23 per cent do this.

| | |
|---|---|
| be **at home** | **work from home** |
| **go home** at … | **leave for work** at … |
| **get to work** at … | **get home** at … |
| **go to work** by bus, by train … | be **at work** |
| be **off work** | |

1 Marc _goes_ to work by car – he drives to work.

2 He _____ _____ work at 7.45 every morning.

3 He _____ _____ _____ at about 8.15 am.

4 He's _____ _____ all day – he doesn't leave the school.

5 He's never ill, so he's never _____ work.

6 Marc _____ home at 6 in the evening. He _____ home at 6.30.

7 But Fiona _____ from home. She's _____ home all day.

● More information:
Vocabulary builder
pages 100–101

▶ More practice:
Workbook page 30

Your turn **B** Work in pairs. Ask and answer the questions.

1 How do you go to work/college?  *I take the train.*

2 What time do you leave for work/college?

3 What time do you get to work/college?

4 When do you go home?

5 What time do you get home?

## Grammar — adverbs

*Marc is **never** ill.*

People **usually** start work at about 9 and go home at 6, but the boss **often** stays later.

I **never** go out for lunch. I **always** have sandwiches at my desk. Lunch isn't important!

Shops are open all day from 9 till 7 or 8 in the evening, **sometimes** later.

I **never** go out in the evening during the week – I'm too tired! I **usually** stay at home and watch television.

■ More information:
Grammar overview
page 113

**A** 13.1 **Listen and complete what Fiona says about her day.**

I try to work regular hours, from ¹ __8__ to 5.30. But when there's a lot to do, I sometimes work in the evenings. For lunch, I have a sandwich.

In France, people in companies usually start work at ² _____ or ³ _____ . They finish at ⁴ _____ or ⁵ _____ . They work 35 hours a week, but managers usually work longer. Lunch is very important and there's a long lunch break. I never phone people in companies in France between ⁶ _____ and ⁷ _____ .

Here, the shops close at ⁸ _____ . They open again at about ⁹ _____ . Then they stay open quite late, until ¹⁰ _____ or ¹¹ _____ .

 Your turn

**B** **Work in pairs. Talk about:**

- when you start and finish work.
  *I usually work from 8 to 5.*
- when shops in your country open and close.
- when people have lunch.

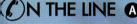

## ON THE LINE

**A** 13.2 **Fiona's brother Douglas lives in Scotland. He is planning a trip to France to visit Fiona. Listen to Douglas making a reservation on the ferry and complete the information.**

| Reservation | |
|---|---|
| first name: *Douglas* | departure date: *10th June* |
| surname: *Macpherson* | departure time: *2.00 pm* |
| make of car: *Renault* | payment amount: _____ |
| model of car: *Laguna* | payment method: cheque / credit card |
| number: _____ | type of card: _____ |
| no. of adults: _____ children: _____ | card no.: _____ |

Your turn

**B** 13.3 **Listen to how Cheryl checks the details with Douglas and complete the conversation.**

**Cheryl:** So, to check the details. Your surname is Macpherson – _____

**Douglas:** That's _____ .

**Cheryl:** You're travelling with a _____ _____ – two _____ , two _____ , on the _____ of June at _____ .

**Douglas:** Right.

**Cheryl:** The number of the car is _____ .

**Douglas:** _____ .

**Cheryl:** And you're paying by _____ , card number _____

**C** **Work in pairs. Repeat the conversation in exercise B, then end it suitably.**

## Checklist

✓ talk about work and home:
*He leaves for work at 7.45.*

✓ adverbs *always, usually, often, sometimes, never*:
*I never go out for lunch.*

✓ check information:
*Your surname is Macpherson.*
*– That's right.*

## present continuous: talking about the future

*We're staying in a hotel in York.*

You can use the present continuous to talk about plans for the future, for example travel plans.

**A** 🔵 *14.1* **Douglas phones Fiona about the trip to France. Listen and answer the questions.**

1 Are they driving from Aberdeen to Dover in one go?   *No, they aren't.*
2 Where are they stopping on the way?
3 Where are they staying in York?
4 Where are they staying in Versailles?
5 When are they arriving at Fiona's house?

**B** **Now practise saying the questions and answers in pairs.**

**A:** *Are they driving from Aberdeen to Dover in one go?*
**B:** *No, they aren't.*

**A** **Look at Fiona's diary and correct the mistake.**

| June | June |
|---|---|
| **11** *Monday* | **14** *Thursday* |
| AM Work on package design for Sigma. | AM Continue with Noval logo project. |
| PM Work on package design for Sigma. | PM Free |
| **12** *Tuesday* | **15** *Friday* |
| AM Finish package design for Sigma. Clean office! | AM Continue with Noval logo project. |
| PM Free. Douglas and family arriving. | PM Continue with Noval logo project. |
| **13** *Wednesday* | **16** *Saturday* |
| AM Work on Noval logo project. | AM Free. Douglas  PM Free and family leaving. |
| PM Visit Michelle Dulac in the Biarritz tourist office. | **17** *Sunday*  AM        PM |

**B** **In another phone call, Douglas asks Fiona about her plans for next week. Complete the conversation.**

**Douglas:** *What ¹ are  you doing on Monday next week?*
**Fiona:** *In the morning and the afternoon, I'm ² _____ on a design project for a company called Sigma. And in the evening you're ³ _____ .*
**Douglas:** *What are you doing on Tuesday?*
**Fiona:** *In the morning ⁴ _____ finishing the Sigma project, and in the afternoon I'm free, so we can do something together.*
**Douglas:** *What about Wednesday?*
**Fiona:** *In the morning I'm ⁵ _____ on a project for a company called Noval.*
**Douglas:** *And in the afternoon?*
**Fiona:** *I'm ⁶ _____ someone at the tourist office in Biarritz.*

**C** 🔵 *14.2* **Now listen, check and repeat.**

**Your turn** **D** Now talk about Fiona.

*On Monday, she's working on the design for Sigma.*

## Grammar 2   irregular plurals

**A** Complete the table.

| | | | |
|---|---|---|---|
| man | *men* | _____ | families |
| *woman* | women | diary | _____ |
| child | _____ | _____ | boxes |
| _____ | people | watch | _____ |

■ More information:
Grammar overview
page 111

**B** [14.3] Now listen, check and repeat.

## ON THE LINE

**A** [14.4] Douglas phones a hotel to make a reservation. Listen and complete the information.

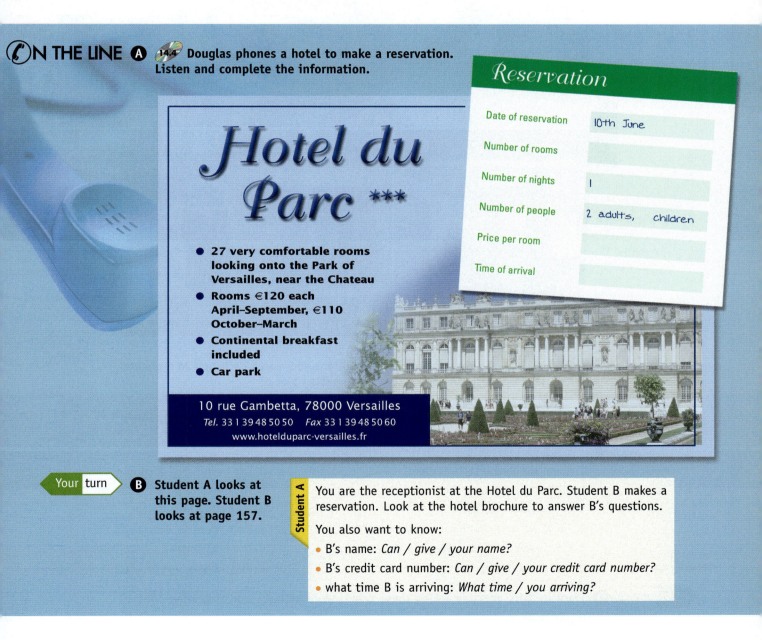

## Reservation

| | |
|---|---|
| Date of reservation | 10th June |
| Number of rooms | |
| Number of nights | 1 |
| Number of people | 2 adults,   children |
| Price per room | |
| Time of arrival | |

## Hotel du Parc ***

- **27 very comfortable rooms looking onto the Park of Versailles, near the Chateau**
- **Rooms €120 each April–September, €110 October–March**
- **Continental breakfast included**
- **Car park**

10 rue Gambetta, 78000 Versailles
*Tel.* 33 1 39 48 50 50    *Fax* 33 1 39 48 50 60
www.hotelduparc-versailles.fr

**Your turn** **B** Student A looks at this page. Student B looks at page 157.

**Student A**
You are the receptionist at the Hotel du Parc. Student B makes a reservation. Look at the hotel brochure to answer B's questions.

You also want to know:

- B's name: *Can / give / your name?*
- B's credit card number: *Can / give / your credit card number?*
- what time B is arriving: *What time / you arriving?*

## Checklist

✓ use the present continuous for future plans: *We're arriving on Monday.*

✓ irregular plurals: *children, people, diaries …*

✓ make hotel reservations by phone: *I'd like to make a reservation, please.*

41

# 15 Can we order, please?

**A**

WE REGRET TO INFORM PASSENGERS THAT THE 2PM FERRY TO CALAIS IS CANCELLED. WE APOLOGISE FOR ANY INCONVIENIENCE. PLAESE WAIT FOR THE 4PM FERRY.

**B**

The restaurant is full this evening. Please try our other restaurant – 23 rue Mazarin.

*Le Petit Zinc* RESTAURANT

**C**

HOTEL

Hotel closed.
There is a problem with the electricity.

If you have a reservation, please go to Hotel Excelsior
→
200 metres.

**A** 🔵 **15.1** Listen to the three pairs of conversations and match each pair to a picture. Which is more polite in each case – conversation a or b?

**B** Work in pairs. Listen again to the polite conversations and practise saying them.

**C** You are at a restaurant. Match the questions to the answers.

1 Could we have a table for four?
2 Please could we see the menu?
3 Can we order, please?
4 Could we have another bottle of wine?
5 Can I have the bill, please?
6 And can I have a receipt, please?

a The menu? Just a minute.
b You'd like to order? What can I get you?
c A receipt? No problem.
d More wine? Of course.
e The bill? Certainly. Here you are.
f Do you have a reservation?

▶ More practice: Workbook page 34

 Your turn

**D** Work in pairs. Practise asking these things more politely, and answering politely.

**Hotel check-in**

1 Carry my bags.
   **A:** *Could you carry my bags, please?*
   **B:** *Of course.*

2 Send a cheese sandwich up to my room.

3 I want to order a newspaper for tomorrow morning – *Le Monde*.

4 I want to check out.

## Reading and vocabulary

**A** Read the extracts from Douglas's diary.

> The hotel in York was closed because there was no electricity. There was another hotel, but the beds were very uncomfortable, and it was difficult to sleep.

> The 2 o'clock ferry from Dover was cancelled because of bad weather. There was another ferry at 4 o'clock, but it was one hour late in Calais.

> The first restaurant in Versailles was full. There was another restaurant next door, but there weren't many people: it was almost empty. I understand why – the food was terrible!

**B** Circle the correct word.

1 If there are no tables free in a restaurant, it is (full) / empty.
2 If the 7 o'clock bus leaves at 6.55, it is early / late.
3 If the bed in your hotel is comfortable / uncomfortable, you can't sleep.
4 If you can go into a shop and buy something, the shop is open / closed.
5 If a ferry, train or bus does not leave, it is late / cancelled.

## Grammar  *was/were*

*The restaurant **was** full.*

**A** Complete the table.

| I/ _He_ /She/It We/You/ _____ | _was_ _____ | on time. |
| Was Were | I/ _____ /she/it _____ /you/they | busy? |
| I/He/She/ _____ We/You/ _____ | wasn't (was not) _____ (were not) | comfortable. |

- More information: Grammar overview page 106
- More practice: Workbook page 35

## ON THE LINE

**A** 🔊 15.2 Douglas phones Fiona. Listen and find out what Douglas says about the following.

1 the hotel in York   *The hotel in York was closed.*
2 the ferry
3 the restaurant yesterday evening
4 the hotel last night

**Your turn 1**

**B** Work in pairs. Student A looks at this page. Student B looks at page 157.

**Student A**

You are going to see a friend in another country (Student B). Phone your friend.

Answer your friend's questions about:
- the trip.   *The train was on time.*
- the restaurant yesterday evening (number of people, food).
- the hotel last night.

## Checklist

✔ ask for things politely: *Can I have the bill, please?*

✔ answer politely when people ask for things: *Certainly. Here you are.*

✔ adjectives: *comfortable, uncomfortable ...*

✔ was/were: *The restaurant was full.*

# 16 I decided to move to France

## Reading

**A** **Read the text.**

### Working from home

More and more people are working from home. A lot of them can choose where they want to live and work. Fiona Macpherson is British but she lives and works in France.

Fiona grew up on the Isle of Skye in Scotland. She went to a design school in Glasgow. Then she worked in a design company for ten years. After that she worked from home for four years. 'Glasgow's an excellent place to work,' she says, 'but I needed a change, so I decided to move to France. I already had a lot of customers in the UK and in Europe. I wanted to find somewhere nice and quiet, with good weather in the summer.'

'I went to France for the first time when I was a student. I knew the Pyrenees well, so I bought a house in a little village called Barcus. It's about 40 kilometres from Pau. I met my husband Marc after I moved here.'

**B** **Now write _T_ (true) or _F_ (false).**

1 Fiona lives in Glasgow. ___F___
2 She grew up on the Isle of Skye. _____
3 She went to a design school in London. _____
4 She worked in a design company for ten years. _____
5 She worked from home in Glasgow for seven years. _____
6 She moved to France because she wanted a change. _____
7 She bought a house in the Pyrenees. _____
8 She met her husband in Scotland. _____

## Grammar

### past simple

*Fiona **grew up** on the Isle of Skye.*
*Fiona **met** her husband in France.*

You can use the past simple to talk about events completed in the past.
The past simple is the same for all persons.

You ask questions with *Did* and the base form of the verb. You make negatives with *didn't* (and the base form of the verb).
**Did** *Fiona* grow *up in France? No, she* **didn't**.

**A** **Complete the table.**

| Regular verbs | | Irregular verbs | |
|---|---|---|---|
| like | liked | buy | bought |
| move | _____ | do | _____ |
| decide | _____ | _____ | had |
| _____ | needed | _____ | went |

**B** **16.1** **Now listen, check and repeat.**

**C** **Complete the sentences with the past simple forms of the verbs in brackets.**

1 Fiona _grew_ _up_ (grow up) on Skye, but she _____ _____ (not stay) there.
2 She _____ (study) in Glasgow. She _____ _____ (not want) to go to London.
3 Fiona _____ (get) a job at a design company, but she _____ _____ (not like) her boss.
4 Then she _____ (work) from home for four years, but she _____ _____ (not feel) lonely.
5 She _____ (buy) a house in the south-west of France. She _____ _____ (not move) to Paris.

■ More information: Grammar overview pages 106–107
◆ List of irregular verbs: page 110

44

**D** 🔵 **16.2** Now listen, check and repeat.

**E** Make questions about Fiona.

1 grow up / Isle of Skye    *Did she grow up on the Isle of Skye?*
2 go / design school / Glasgow
3 work from home / four years
4 move / big city / France
5 buy / house / Alps
6 know / Pyrenees / before / move / there

**F** Now practise saying the questions and answers in pairs.

**A:** *Did Fiona go to a design school in Glasgow?*       **A:** *Did she move to a big city in France?*
**B:** *Yes, she did.*                                                           **B:** *No, she didn't. She moved to a small village.*

**G** 🔵 **16.3** Now listen, check and repeat.

**Reading and writing**

**A** Last year, a company called Work Research wrote a report about homeworking.
Read the report and write sentences about homeworkers last year, using the past simple.

*44 per cent of homeworkers were consultants.*

*73 per cent of homeworkers drank too much coffee.*

*For 48 per cent, the main advantage was independence.*

## HOMEWORKERS ...

| | | | | |
|---|---|---|---|---|
| are consultants. | 44% | | drink too much coffee. | 73% |
| are designers. | 18% | | do not drink too much coffee. | 27% |
| have other jobs. | 38% | | | |
| | | | work in their pyjamas. | 17% |
| have a special office. | 76% | | never work in their pyjamas. | 83% |
| work somewhere else. | 24% | | | |
| | | | work in the evenings. | 88% |
| eat too much. | 64% | | never work in the evenings. | 12% |
| do not eat too much. | 36% | | | |

| The main advantage is ... | | The main disadvantage is ... | |
|---|---|---|---|
| independence. | 48% | not enough contact with colleagues. | 56% |
| not travelling to work. | 25% | it's difficult to separate work and free time. | 28% |
| something else. | 27% | something else | 16% |

**Listening and speaking**

**A** 🔵 **16.4** Douglas and his family arrive at Fiona's house. Listen and match Fiona's questions to their answers.

1 Did you find the house OK?                     **a** No, not a lot.
2 Did you have a good journey?                   **b** No, we had a sandwich.
3 Did you stop for lunch?                              **c** After Versailles, it was very easy.
4 Did you bring a lot of luggage?                **d** No problem.

 **B** Work in pairs. Student A looks at this page. Student B looks at page 157.

**Student A**
Student B comes to visit you. Ask questions 1–4 from exercise A.

**Checklist**  ✔ regular and irregular verbs in the past simple: *Did you have a good journey?*    ✔ homeworking: *The main advantage was independence.*

**Reading** **A** Read the letter Fiona received on Tuesday morning (the day after Douglas arrived).

Macpherson Designs
2 rue du Canon
64130 Barcus

 Midi Editions

Friday 8th June

Dear Ms Macpherson,

I think you agreed to send the designs for the cover of *The Wonderful Pyrenees* by Wednesday 6th. I am writing this letter to you because you did not answer my e-mails – perhaps you didn't get them. It is now Friday, and your designs are still not here. Did you finish the designs? Did you send them? This is very urgent. Please could you contact me as soon as possible.

Looking forward to hearing from you,

Yours sincerely,

*Magali Martin*

Magali Martin

120 rue Royal, 31000 Toulouse  Tel: +33 (0)5 61 97 73 00  Fax: +33 (0)5 61 97 73 10

**B** Now write *T* (true) or *F* (false).

1 Magali Martin sent the letter on 8th June. __T__

2 Fiona agreed to send the designs by Thursday last week. _____

3 Fiona answered Magali Martin's e-mails last week. _____

4 Magali says that the designs are very urgent. _____

5 Magali is waiting to hear from Fiona. _____

**Listening** **A** 🔊 *17.1* It's Tuesday evening. When Fiona comes in, she finds four messages on her answering machine. Listen and match the callers to the subjects of their messages.

1 Amanda Lee-Smith, Pocket Books    **a** designs that did not arrive

2 Jacques Lebrun, Sigma    **b** meeting on Wednesday

3 Michelle Dulac, Biarritz tourist office    **c** cover design

4 Magali Martin, Midi Editions    **d** package design

**☎N THE LINE** **A** 🔊 *17.2* Listen to the conversation between Fiona and Magali Martin and answer the questions.

1 Did Magali phone Fiona?   *No, she didn't. Fiona phoned Magali.*

2 Did Fiona get Magali's letter?

3 Did Fiona get her e-mails?

4 Did Fiona send her designs? Why/Why not?

5 What do they agree?

**Your turn** **B** Work in pairs. Student A looks at this page. Student B looks at page 157.

**Student A** You are Fiona. Phone Amanda Lee-Smith of Pocket Books (Student B) about some designs you sent last week. Use the information below to answer her questions. Then end the conversation.

- You sent the designs on Monday by express post.
- You didn't receive any e-mails from her.
- You can send the designs again – you have other copies.

## Writing

**A** Fiona writes a letter to Amanda Lee-Smith with copies of the designs. Complete Fiona's letter with the correct forms of the verbs in brackets.

**MD** *Macpherson Designs*

2 rue du Canon
64130 Barcus
Tel +33 (0)5 59 28 30 25     Fax +33 (0)5 59 28 30 27
E-mail: macpherson.designs
@zapmail.com

Amanda Lee-Smith
Pocket Books
12 Broad Street
Oxford OX1 3DF
United Kingdom

13 June

Dear Amanda,

I'm sorry you didn't get the designs. As I said on the phone, I sent them by post last week. Here [1] _are_ (be) some copies of the same designs.

Please can you [2] _____ (send) me an e-mail to say that you [3] _____ (get) them OK.

I [4] _____ (hope) that you [5] _____ (like) the designs.

I'm [6] _____ (come) to London at the end of June.

I hope that we [7] _____ (can) meet then.

I'm [8] _____ (look) forward to [9] _____ (hear) from you.

Yours sincerely,

*Fiona*

## Reading and speaking

**A** Fiona and Douglas went to Biarritz on Wednesday afternoon. Read the beginning of the conversation they had when they got back.

**Fiona**

> I got a letter from a client in Toulouse yesterday. She wasn't very happy.

**Douglas**

> What was the problem?

**B** Now put the rest of the conversation in order.

**a** ☐
> It's a book called 'The Wonderful Pyrenees'. I'm designing the cover.

**e** ☐
> Don't mention it!

**b** ☐
> Great idea! Biarritz with the Pyrenees behind – an excellent picture for the cover. Thanks, Douglas!

**f** ☐
> We went to Biarritz today. Did you think of using pictures of Biarritz? It's beautiful.

**c** ☐
> Because I didn't send them. I didn't know what to put in the designs.

**g** ☐
> Why not?

**d** ☑ 3
> She didn't get some designs by a deadline that we agreed.

**h** ☐
> What's the project?

**Your turn**   **C** Now practise saying the conversation in pairs.

## Checklist

✓ deadlines: *You agreed to send the designs by Wednesday.*

✓ expressions: *I'm looking forward to hearing from you.*

47

# 18 Where did you go?

## Listening

**A** 🔘 18.1 After Douglas and his family leave, Fiona sends the designs for *The Wonderful Pyrenees* to Magali Martin. They arrive by the deadline, Tuesday. On Thursday, Fiona goes to see her. Listen to the conversation and complete the sentences.

1 Fiona went by _car_ to Toulouse.
2 Her journey took _____ hours.
3 Fiona drank _____ at the meeting.

4 Magali liked Fiona's photos for the _____ design.
5 She asked Fiona if she wanted to take photos for the whole _____ .

## Grammar

**past simple with question words**

*How long did it take?*

**A** Complete the past simple questions, using the question words in the box.

| Who | When | Why | What | How | ~~Where~~ | How long |

1 _Where_ did you go yesterday?        I went to Toulouse.
2 _____ did you get there?             I drove.
3 _____ did you see?                   Magali Martin at Midi Editions.
4 _____ did you see her?               To talk about a book on the Pyrenees.
5 _____ _____ did the meeting take?    About two hours.
6 _____ did you agree?                 I agreed to take the photos for the book.
7 _____ did you get back?              About 6 o'clock.

**B** 🔘 18.2 Now listen, check and repeat.

▶ More practice: Workbook page 40

**C** Work in pairs. Practise saying the questions and answers in exercise A.

## ON THE LINE

**A** 🔘 18.3 After the meeting, Fiona receives an e-mail from Magali Martin. Listen to the conversation and complete Fiona's notes about the things she disagrees with.

1 _Wonderful_
2 _____
3 _____
4 _____

From:     ‹magali.martin@midi-editions.fr›
To:       ‹macpherson.designs@zapmail.com.›
Date:     22 June 200-
Subject:  Book project
_____

Dear Ms Macpherson

Thank you for coming to see me yesterday about The [1]*Beautiful Pyrenees* – it was a very useful meeting.

We want to work with you on this project – the cover design, the photos and [2]~~the text~~ for the whole book. Deadlines for your work are as follows:

Delivery of final cover design: [3]~~1 month~~

Delivery of photos for the book: [4]~~3~~ months

If you agree to these conditions, I can send you a contract.

Best wishes,

Magali Martin

**Your turn** ▶ **B** Work in pairs. Fiona Macpherson phones Magali Martin. Practise saying the first part of their conversation.

**A:** *Hello. This is Fiona Macpherson.*

**B:** *Hello, Fiona. Did you get my e-mail OK?*

**A:** *Yes thanks, but I'm afraid there are a few mistakes in it.*

**B:** *I'm sorry to hear that. What are they?*

**C** Work in pairs. Fiona uses the notes she made in exercise A to talk about the e-mail. Magali agrees with Fiona about all the points. Continue their conversation.

**A:** *I thought the title of the book was 'The Wonderful Pyrenees', but you put 'The Beautiful Pyrenees'.*

**B:** *You're right – it is 'The Wonderful Pyrenees'.*

…

**D** Work in pairs. Magali apologises for the mistakes and Fiona accepts her apologies. Practise reading what they say.

**B:** *I'm sorry about the mistakes.*

**A:** *That's all right.*

**E** Work in pairs. End the conversation politely.

---

**Writing** **A** After the call, Magali Martin writes an e-mail to Fiona.
Complete the e-mail with the correct forms of the verbs in brackets.

From: ‹magali.martin@midi-editions.fr›
To: ‹macpherson.designs@zapmail.com›
Date: 22 June 200-
Subject: The Wonderful Pyrenees book

Dear Ms Macpherson,

Thank you for your phone call.

I [1] *am* (be) sorry that there [2] *was* (be) a misunderstanding about what we [3] *decided* (decide).

You [4] _____ (be) right about all the points. Delivery of the final cover design [5] _____ (be) in two months, and delivery of the photos [6] _____ (be) in five months. Someone else [7] _____ (do) the text.

I [8] _____ (send) the contract to you today. Please [9] _____ (can) you return it as soon as possible.

Best wishes,

Magali Martin

---

**Checklist** ✓ past simple with question words: *Who did you see?*   ✓ check information: *I'm sure we said one month.*   ✓ expressions: *Please can you return it as soon as possible.*

# Review 13–18

**A** Correct the sentences. In each sentence, there is
• one word too many OR • one word missing OR • one wrong word.

**1** Stanislas leaves for the work at 6.30 every morning.
*Stanislas leaves for work at 6.30 every morning.*

**2** He never to work by car – he always takes the train.
*He never goes to work by car – he always takes the train.*

**3** He gets at work at about 7.15.
*He gets to work at about 7.15.*

**4** He's at the work all day.

**5** He's never ill, so he's never out work.

**6** He home in the evening at about 6.00.

**7** His wife Anna works from the home.

**8** She at home in the morning and she goes out in the afternoon for a walk.

**9** She home from her walk at 4.30.

**B** Complete the sentences with the correct forms of the verbs in brackets.

**1** Marc always drives (drive) to work. He never takes (take) the bus. There is no bus!

**2** Fiona _____ _____ (not phone) clients in the evening, but sometimes she _____ (write) e-mails to them.

**3** Marc and Fiona never _____ (talk) about work.

**4** Fiona usually _____ (finish) projects on time.

**5** Fiona _____ _____ (not work) in a company, but sometimes she _____ (visit) companies.

**6** Fiona _____ _____ (not like) to work at weekends.

**7** Marc always _____ (teach) on Saturday mornings.

**8** In France, a lot of children _____ (go) to school on Saturday mornings, but in England children _____ _____ (not go) to school on Saturdays.

**C** Work in pairs. Student A looks at this page. Student B looks at page 157.

**Student A**

You bought a ferry ticket (Gothenburg to Harwich) from a travel company, but you want to change it.

- Phone and speak to the person who sold you the ticket, Student B.
- Tell them the changes you want to make.
- Agree to pay the difference between the old price and the new price (by Visa 4408 0412 3456 7890).
- End the conversation politely.

**Old details**

Reservation

```
Volvo 370 – Number: DPT 943
driver and two other people
leave on 1st  August, 9.00 pm
price: 455 euros
```

**New details**

Reservation

```
Saab 95 – Number: FLG 825
driver and three other people
leave on 3rd  August, 8.00 am
new price: 500 euros
```

**D** **Complete Fiona's e-mail with the correct forms of the verbs in brackets. (Check the verb list on page 110.)**

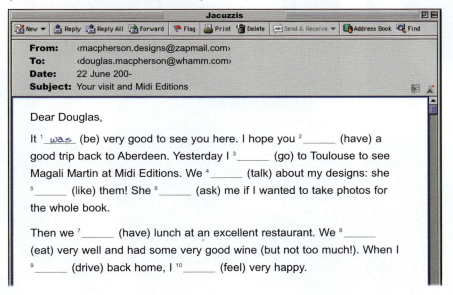

**From:** ‹macpherson.designs@zapmail.com›
**To:** ‹douglas.macpherson@whamm.com›
**Date:** 22 June 200-
**Subject:** Your visit and Midi Editions

Dear Douglas,

It ¹ _was_ (be) very good to see you here. I hope you ² _____ (have) a good trip back to Aberdeen. Yesterday I ³ _____ (go) to Toulouse to see Magali Martin at Midi Editions. We ⁴ _____ (talk) about my designs: she ⁵ _____ (like) them! She ⁶ _____ (ask) me if I wanted to take photos for the whole book.

Then we ⁷ _____ (have) lunch at an excellent restaurant. We ⁸ _____ (eat) very well and had some very good wine (but not too much!). When I ⁹ _____ (drive) back home, I ¹⁰ _____ (feel) very happy.

**E** **Complete the crossword.**

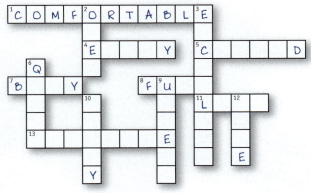

**Across**
1 You can sleep well in this bed: it's very ... (11)
4 There was no one on the train. It was ... (5)
5 We went to the shop but couldn't go in. It was ... (6)
7 I'm very ... I have a lot of work to do. (4)
8 There are no rooms at the hotel. It's ... (4)
11 The traffic was very bad and I was two hours ... for the meeting. (4)
13 very bad (8)

**Down**
2 not closed (4)
3 very good (9)
6 Cities are noisy, but villages are usually ... (5)
9 Can you deliver this today? It's very ... (6)
10 not late, but ... (5)
12 not early, not late, but on ... (4)

**F** **Use some of the words and expressions from Units 13–18 to talk or write about yourself or the characters and situations.**

*I live in the country. It's very quiet!*

*I don't like e-mail. I prefer to use the phone.*

*Fiona works from home, but I could never do that. I need colleagues!*

MODULE

4

SUPERSPORT

Astrid Schmidt works for Supersport, a big European chain of sports stores. Supersport opens new stores in the US, but the California store has low sales. Astrid tries to solve this problem.

# 19  Supersport has arrived

| Grammar | present perfect |
| Vocabulary | company departments |
| On the line | recorded information |

> **Which department do you work or study in?**

# 20  Do you have any tents?

| Grammar | *some; any* |
| Vocabulary | adjectives to describe products |
| On the line | making enquiries about products |

> **Who answers enquiries in your organisation?**

# 21  The service was slow

| Vocabulary | service; numbers 600–999 |
| On the line | percentages |

> **Are people working in a) shops and b) government departments usually friendly?**

# 22  The smallest company

| Grammar | comparatives and superlatives |
| Vocabulary | markets and competitors; numbers: thousands, millions, billions |

> **Think of a company you like. What's its biggest competitor?**

# 23  You must improve training

| Grammar | *must* |
| On the line | confirming arrangements |
| Writing | an e-mail to confirm arrangements |

> **What must you do today?**

# 24  Follow my advice

| Grammar | *advise, want, tell; agree, disagree* |
| On the line | making a suggestion |
| Writing | a report to head office |

> **If someone gives you advice, do you follow it?**

 Review 19–24

**Reading** Ⓐ **Read the newspaper article.**

# SUPERSPORT MOVES INTO THE US MARKET

> Americans spend $21 billion on sporting goods every year.

Supersport is a big European chain of sports stores. Now it has arrived in the United States. Astrid Schmidt of Supersport Europe has moved to New York to manage its American activities. She says, 'We've studied the United States market. It's a difficult market. We've only been in the US for a year. We've invested a lot of money – $400 million – but we're sure we've made the right decision. We've built nine stores in New England and one in California. We plan to open stores in other areas of the US too.'

Ⓑ **Now write *T* (true) or *F* (false).**

1 Supersport is an American company. ___F___

2 Astrid Schmidt has moved to New York. _____

3 She thinks the US is an easy market for Supersport. _____

4 They have invested a lot of money in the US. _____

5 They have built nine stores in New England and two in California. _____

6 They plan to open other stores too. _____

## Grammar present perfect

**We've** (We have) **built** nine stores in New England.

You can use the present perfect to talk about things in the recent past.

You make the present perfect with *have* or *has* and the past participle.

**A** **Complete the sentences with the present perfect forms of the verbs in brackets.**

1 Supersport <u>has  arrived</u> (arrive) in the US.
2 They _____ _____ (invest) a lot of money.
3 They _____ _____ (build) a new store in California.
4 They _____ _____ (make) the right decision.

**B** **Complete the table with the base forms of the verbs or the past participles.**

| Regular verbs | | Irregular verbs | |
|---|---|---|---|
| arrive | <u>arrived</u> | build | <u>built</u> |
| invest | _____ | make | _____ |
| _____ | moved | _____ | sold |

**C** **19.1  Now listen, check and repeat.**

**D** **Work in pairs. Student A looks at this page. Student B looks at page 158.**

More information:
Grammar overview pages 107–108

List of irregular verbs: page 110

More practice: Workbook page 44

**Student A**

You are a journalist. Ask Astrid Schmidt (Student B) these questions, using the present perfect forms of the verbs in brackets.

1 you (move) / New York   *Have you moved to New York?*
2 Supersport (make) / right decision   *Has Supersport made the right decision?*
3 many stores / Supersport (built) / the US
4 Supersport (invest) a lot of money
5 Supersport (open) too many stores

## Vocabulary

**A** **Match the company departments to the things they do.**

1 sales
2 accounts
3 human resources
4 production
5 planning

a pay employees, find and interview new employees, etc
b sell the company's products
c make the company's products
d make plans for the company's future
e deal with money coming into and going out of the company

## ON THE LINE

**A** **19.2  Listen to Supersport's recorded telephone message. Which number do you press if you want to speak to the following?**

1 Astrid Schmidt   _4_
2 the accounts department _____
3 the planning department _____
4 the human resources department _____

Your **turn**

**B** **Imagine that your organisation has a similar recorded message. Complete the message, using the names of departments in the box.**

| accounts   human resources   order enquiries |
| production     sales |

Welcome to _____ . For _____ , press one. For _____ , press two. If you want to _____ , please press _____ . For all other enquiries, please _____ .

## Checklist

✓ present perfect: *We've studied the US market.*

✓ company departments: *sales, production …*

✓ recorded information: *For all other enquiries, please hold.*

**Vocabulary**

Ⓐ Read about the tents that Supersport sells.

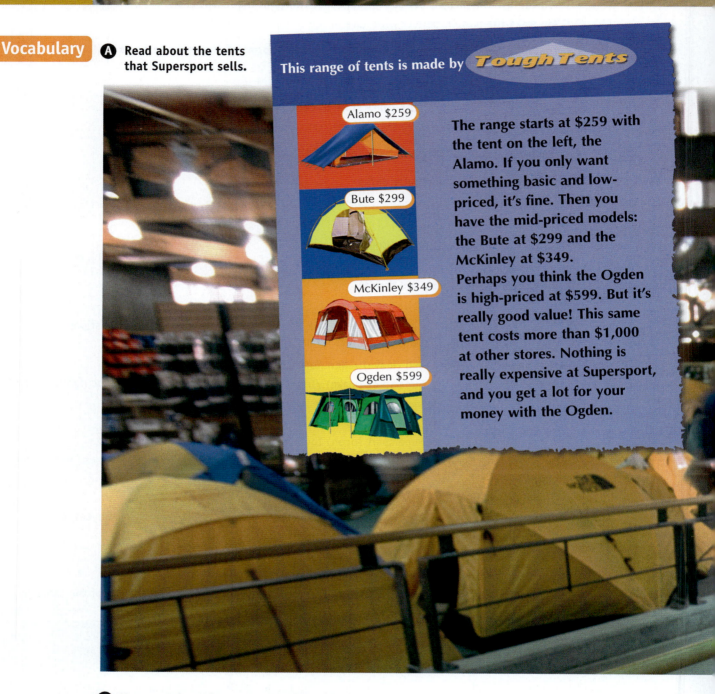

This range of tents is made by **Tough Tents**

Alamo $259

Bute $299

McKinley $349

Ogden $599

The range starts at $259 with the tent on the left, the Alamo. If you only want something basic and low-priced, it's fine. Then you have the mid-priced models: the Bute at $299 and the McKinley at $349.
Perhaps you think the Ogden is high-priced at $599. But it's really good value! This same tent costs more than $1,000 at other stores. Nothing is really expensive at Supersport, and you get a lot for your money with the Ogden.

Ⓑ Now complete the sentences about the tents.

1 The range starts at _$259_ .

2 The _____ is the basic model.

3 The _____ and the _____ are mid-priced.

4 The Ogden is good _____ .

**Listening**

Ⓐ 🔵20.1 Listen to the five conversations and check if these things are in stock.

| BIKES | | TENTS | | JACKETS | | BOOTS | | MAPS | |
|-------|-----|-------|-----|---------|-----|-------|-----|------|-----|
| Armstrong | _yes_ | Alamo | _____ | X500 | _____ | Austrian | _____ | Colombia | _____ |
| Lemond | _no_ | Bute | _____ | X600 | _____ | Italian | _____ | Ecuador | _____ |

## Grammar

### *some; any*

*Do you have **any** maps of South America?*

*– We have **some** maps of Peru, but we don't have **any** maps of Brazil.*

You can use *some* and *any* to talk about quantities.

**Ⓐ Complete the table.**

|  | affirmative | negative | questions | offers |
|---|---|---|---|---|
| *some* | We have <u>some</u> maps of Ecuador. We have _____ Austrian boots. |  |  | Would you like _____ coffee? |
| *any* |  | We don't have _____ Italian boots. There aren't _____ Alamo tents. | Do you have _____ X500 jackets? Are there _____ American boots in stock? |  |

**Ⓑ 20.2 Now listen, check and repeat.**

**Ⓒ Complete the sentences, using *some* or *any*.**

1 We have <u>some</u> camping tables, but we don't have <u>any</u> chairs. We're out of stock.
2 In the summer, we don't keep _____ skis in stock.
3 We have _____ maps of Colorado, but we don't have _____ maps of Utah right now.
4 We have _____ very good backpacks. Would you like to try _____ of them?
5 We have _____ basic tents, but at the moment we don't have _____ mid-priced tents.

- More information: Grammar overview page 112
- More practice: Workbook page 46

## ON THE LINE

**Ⓐ 20.3 Listen to the four conversations and write down the number of products in stock.**

| 1 bikes | 2 tents | 3 jackets | 4 maps |
|---|---|---|---|
| Simpson __8__ | McKinley _____ | X300 _____ | Brazil _____ |
| Anquetil __0__ | Ogden _____ | X400 _____ | Peru _____ |

**Ⓑ Now listen again and write the number of the conversation in which you hear each expression.**

**Salesperson**

a *I think we have one left.* _2_

b *What size do you take?* ___

c *We're expecting them next week.* ___

**Customer**

d *I want to come in and buy …* ___

e *I'm calling about …* ___

f *Do yo have any …* ___

**Your turn**

**Ⓒ Work in pairs. Student A is the salesperson. Student B is the customer. Use the same expressions in similar conversations about the products in exercise A.**

**A:** *Clothing – how may I help you?*

**B:** *Hi. I want to come in and buy an X400 jacket. Do you have any in stock?*

**A:** *Yes, we have some here – about 12, I think. What size do you take? …*

## Checklist

✓ adjectives to describe products: *low-priced, mid-priced …*

✓ some; any: *We have some camping tables, but we don't have any chairs.*

✓ make enquiries about products: *Do you have any maps of South America?*

**Listening and speaking**

**A** 🔘 **21.1** Supersport asked its customers what they thought of its service and its products. Listen to the four interviews. Which of the words below do you hear? Write the number of the conversation.

| Service | |
|---|---|
| excellent _____ | good _____ |
| slow _____ | helpful _____ |
| poor _____ | fast _____ |
| unhelpful _____ | friendly _____ |
| unfriendly _1_ | |

 **Your turn**

**B** Work in pairs. Ask and answer questions about a shop that you went to recently.

**A:** *What did you buy? Where did you buy it?*
**B:** *I bought a jacket at ...*
**A:** *What did you think of the service?*
**B:** *It was excellent.*

**Reading and vocabulary**

**A** Read the e-mail to Harry Esposito, manager of the Supersport store in Sacramento.

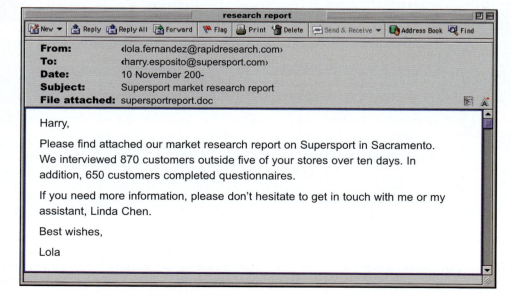

research report

New ▾   Reply   Reply All   Forward   Flag   Print   Delete   Send & Receive ▾   Address Book   Find

**From:** ‹lola.fernandez@rapidresearch.com›
**To:** ‹harry.esposito@supersport.com›
**Date:** 10 November 200-
**Subject:** Supersport market research report
**File attached:** supersportreport.doc

Harry,

Please find attached our market research report on Supersport in Sacramento. We interviewed 870 customers outside five of your stores over ten days. In addition, 650 customers completed questionnaires.

If you need more information, please don't hesitate to get in touch with me or my assistant, Linda Chen.

Best wishes,

Lola

**B** Now answer the questions.

1 Who is the e-mail from?   *Lola Fernandez*

2 Where does Lola Fernandez work?

3 How many people spoke to the researchers?

4 How many customers completed questionnaires?

5 Who is Linda Chen?

6 What can Harry do if he wants more information?

**C**  Listen to the numbers and underline the ones you hear.

■ More information:
Vocabulary builder
page 103

| 600 | 650 | 692 | 700 | 738 | 777 | 787 | 792 |
| 800 | 821 | 843 | 870 | 900 | 950 | 963 | 999 |

**ON THE LINE** **A** 21.3 Harry looks at the report attached to the e-mail from Lola. Some of the figures are missing, so he phones Rapid Research.
Listen to the beginning of the conversation. Complete the figures in the second and third lines of the table.

**Rapid Research Inc.**

### Supersport customer satisfaction report

| | excellent | good | fair | poor |
|---|---|---|---|---|
| Quality of products | 35% | 45% | 15% | 5% |
| Choice of products | 40% | 33% | | |
| Availability of products | 9% | | | |
| Service | 15% | | | |
| The look of the store | 12% | | | |

**Your turn** **B** Work in pairs. Student A looks at this page. Student B looks at page 158.

**Student A**

• You are Harry Esposito. Ask Lola Fernandez (Student B) for the information missing from the last two lines of the table.

A: *What are the figures for service?*

B: *15 per cent of customers think the service is excellent, 25 per cent good ...*

• Thank Lola Fernandez and end the conversation.

A: *Thanks for your help.*

B: *That's all right.*

**Checklist** ✓ talk about service: *The saleswoman was helpful.*  ✓ expressions: *Please find attached ...*  ✓ numbers 600–999  ✓ percentages: *15 per cent of customers think the service is excellent.*

# 22 The smallest company

**Reading** **A** Read the research report.

## The US sporting goods market

The market for sporting goods in the US is very big. Supersport has entered the market only recently: it's the smallest competitor, with ten stores. Sportmart is bigger, with 25 stores, while Aktiv is the biggest company, with 110 stores. Supersport has 450 employees, and Sportmart has 900, but the company with the most employees is Aktiv, with 3,000.

Supersport made a loss of $5 million in its first year in the US, on sales of $250 million. Sportmart had much higher sales of $700 million, and made a profit $60 million. The most profitable company was Aktiv, which made $200 million in profit, on sales of $2 billion.

**B** Now complete the table.

|  | Supersport | Sportmart | Aktiv |
|---|---|---|---|
| stores | 10 |  |  |
| employees |  | 900 |  |
| sales last year |  | $700 million |  |
| profit/loss last year |  |  | $200 million profit |

## Grammar — comparatives and superlatives

*Sportmart is **bigger than** Supersport.*
*Aktiv is **the biggest** company.*

**A** Complete the table.

|  | base form | comparative | superlative |
|---|---|---|---|
| **one syllable** | big | bigger | biggest |
|  | small | ____ | ____ |
| **two or more syllables** | expensive | more expensive | ____ ____ |
|  | profitable | ____ ____ | ____ ____ |
| **irregular** | good | better | ____ |
|  | bad | ____ | ____ |

**B** Talk about the companies in the research report on page 60, using comparatives and superlatives.

**1** big (company) *Sportmart is bigger than Supersport, but Aktiv is the biggest company.*
**2** high (sales)
**3** profitable (company)

- More information:
  Grammar overview
  pages 112–113
- More practice:
  Workbook page 50

## Numbers

*Aktiv has **three thousand** employees.*
*Supersport made a loss of **$5 million**. ($5,000,000)*
*Aktiv had sales of **$2 billion**. ($2,000,000,000)*

*How many products does Supersport sell?* – *Thousands.*
If you don't give an exact number, you say *thousands, millions* or *billions*.

**A** 22.1 Listen to the numbers and <u>underline</u> the ones you hear.

| <u>a thousand</u> | 10,000 | 93,000 | 250,000 | € 800,000 |
|---|---|---|---|---|
| a million | $5 million | 17 million | 70 million | 278 million |
| 7 billion | $21 billion | 54 billion | 87 billion | $500 billion |

**B** Match the questions to the answers. If you don't know, guess!

**1** How many people live in the United States?        **a** 93,000
**2** How many Americans play soccer (= European-type football)?    **b** 17 million
**3** How many Americans go to watch baseball?    **c** 70 million
**4** What was the highest number of people at a baseball match?    **d** $500 billion
**5** How much do Americans spend on sporting goods every year?    **e** 278 million
**6** How much do Americans spend on goods and services for their free time in general?    **f** $21 billion

**C** Answer the questions with *thousands, millions* or *billions*.

**1** How many American school children play soccer?
**2** How many customers does Supersport have in California?
**3** How many people watch soccer on TV around the world?

- More information:
  Vocabulary builder
  page 103

## Checklist

✓ comparatives and superlatives:
*Sportmart is bigger than Supersport.*
*Aktiv is the biggest company.*

✓ markets and competitors:
*market, sales …*

✓ thousands, millions, billions:
*278 million people live in
the United States.*

## Reading

**A** Astrid receives the report from Rapid Research about the Sacramento store. Read the notes that she makes about it.

> ○ Problems at the Sacramento store
>
> ○ 1 Customers are happy with the quality and choice of products. These aren't the problems.
>
> ○ 2 Customers often find that what they want is out of stock. Is there a problem with the computer system for ordering products? We must improve the computer system immediately. This is the main problem.
>
> ○ 3 60% of customers say the service is 'fair' or 'poor'. We must improve staff training.
>
> ○ 4 We must make the look of the store more modern.

**B** Now match the headings to the notes.

○ _2_ STOCK PROBLEMS    ○ __ SERVICE PROBLEMS

○ __ THE LOOK OF THE STORE    ○ __ QUALITY AND CHOICE OF PRODUCTS

**C** What is the worst problem at the Sacramento store?

## Grammar  *must*

▶ More practice: Workbook page 52

We **must** improve the computer system.

You can use *must* to say what is necessary in a direct way.

## ON THE LINE **A** 23.1 Astrid Schmidt in New York phones Harry Esposito in Sacramento.
Listen to the conversation and write sentences to correct Harry's e-mail.

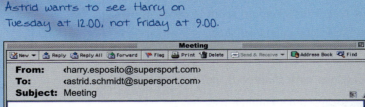
Astrid wants to see Harry on Tuesday at 12.00, not Friday at 9.00.

**Meeting**

New ▾ | Reply | Reply All | Forward | Flag | Print | Delete | Send & Receive ▾ | Address Book | Find

**From:** ‹harry.esposito@supersport.com›
**To:** ‹astrid.schmidt@supersport.com›
**Subject:** Meeting

Astrid,

It was good to talk with you. This is to confirm the arrangements for our meeting on Friday morning at 9.00 in Los Angeles. I can send someone to meet you at the airport. I've asked my PA to reserve a hotel for you for three nights. The hotel is about five miles from the city center.

Best wishes,

Harry

**Writing**

**A** Write the correct version of the e-mail from Harry to Astrid.

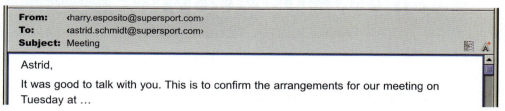

From: ‹harry.esposito@supersport.com›
To: ‹astrid.schmidt@supersport.com›
Subject: Meeting

Astrid,

It was good to talk with you. This is to confirm the arrangements for our meeting on Tuesday at …

**Listening and speaking**

**A** 23.2 Astrid is talking to Harry at their meeting in Sacramento. Listen to the conversation once. Then listen again and complete the conversation. Put the verbs in brackets in the correct form and add other words as necessary.

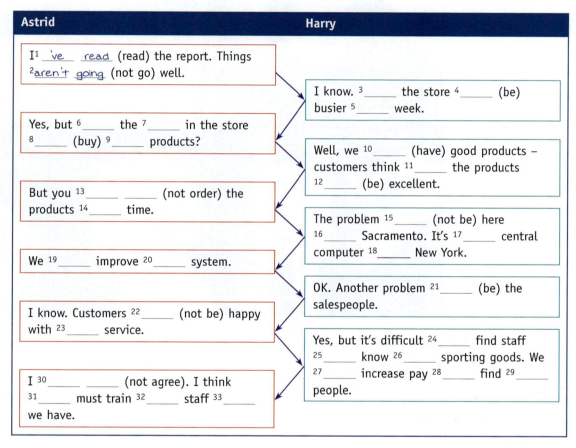

| Astrid | Harry |
|---|---|
| I¹ 've read (read) the report. Things ² aren't going (not go) well. | |
| | I know. ³ _____ the store ⁴ _____ (be) busier ⁵ _____ week. |
| Yes, but ⁶ _____ the ⁷ _____ in the store ⁸ _____ (buy) ⁹ _____ products? | |
| | Well, we ¹⁰ _____ (have) good products – customers think ¹¹ _____ the products ¹² _____ (be) excellent. |
| But you ¹³ _____ _____ (not order) the products ¹⁴ _____ time. | |
| | The problem ¹⁵ _____ (not be) here ¹⁶ _____ Sacramento. It's ¹⁷ _____ central computer ¹⁸ _____ New York. |
| We ¹⁹ _____ improve ²⁰ _____ system. | |
| | OK. Another problem ²¹ _____ (be) the salespeople. |
| I know. Customers ²² _____ (not be) happy with ²³ _____ service. | |
| | Yes, but it's difficult ²⁴ _____ find staff ²⁵ _____ know ²⁶ _____ sporting goods. We ²⁷ _____ increase pay ²⁸ _____ find ²⁹ _____ people. |
| I ³⁰ _____ _____ (not agree). I think ³¹ _____ must train ³² _____ staff ³³ _____ we have. | |

**B** Now practise saying the conversation in pairs.

Your turn **C** Student A looks at this page. Student B looks at page 158.

**Student A**

You are a supermarket manager. Your boss from head office (Student B) phones you to talk about problems in your supermarket.

- Answer politely. Say that it's very difficult to get cleaning staff – the pay (decided by head office) is too low.
  *It's very difficult to find cleaning staff. The pay is too low – they don't want to work here.*
- Say that it's very difficult to find check-out staff: you can only find students, or people waiting to find a 'real' job in another company. Training them is not an answer because they usually leave after 4–6 weeks.
- End the call politely.

**Checklist** ✓ *must: We must improve the system.*     ✓ *expressions: This is to confirm the arrangements for our meeting.*

# 24 Follow my advice

**Reading** **A** After her meeting with Harry Esposito, the store manager at Sacramento, Astrid wrote to the head of Supersport in Frankfurt. Read her e-mail.

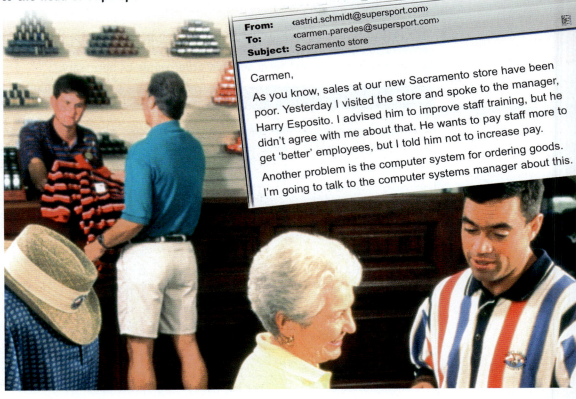

From: ‹astrid.schmidt@supersport.com›
To: ‹carmen.paredes@supersport.com›
Subject: Sacramento store

Carmen,

As you know, sales at our new Sacramento store have been poor. Yesterday I visited the store and spoke to the manager, Harry Esposito. I advised him to improve staff training, but he didn't agree with me about that. He wants to pay staff more to get 'better' employees, but I told him not to increase pay.

Another problem is the computer system for ordering goods. I'm going to talk to the computer systems manager about this.

**B** Now answer the questions.

1 When did Astrid visit the Sacramento store? *Yesterday.*

2 What did she advise Harry to do?

3 Did he agree?

4 What does he want to do?

5 Does Astrid agree?

6 Who is Astrid going to talk to about the computer systems?

**Grammar** ***advise, want, tell; agree, disagree***

I **advised him to** improve staff training.
He **disagreed** with me.

**A** Look at these verb patterns.

advise
ask ⎫
tell ⎬ someone to do something
want ⎭

agree ⎫
disagree ⎬ with someone

**B** Write complete sentences with the correct forms of the verbs in brackets.

1 Astrid (advise) Harry (improve) staff training.
*Astrid advised Harry to improve staff training.*

2 Harry (disagree) with her.

3 Astrid (tell) him (keep) pay the same.

4 Astrid (want) the computer systems manager (phone) her.

5 She (ask) him (go) to Sacramento.

- More information: Grammar overview page 109
▶ More practice: Workbook page 54

# ☏N THE LINE

**A** 🔵 24.1 Jim Green is the manager of Supersport's central computer system in New York. Astrid asks him to phone her. Listen and put the parts of their conversation in order.

| Astrid | Jim |
|---|---|
| ☐ **a** Ask Jim to come to discuss the suggestion in more detail. | Confirm and say goodbye. **i** ☐ |
| ☐ **b** Say there are problems with the stock, and what they are. | Accept. **j** ☐ |
| ☐ **c** Say what the suggestion is. | Say what you think the real problem is. **k** ☐ |
| 1 **d** Answer with your name. | React. **l** ☐ |
| ☐ **e** Say where you went yesterday. | Ask how it's going there. **m** ☐ |
| ☐ **f** Say goodbye. | React. **n** ☐ |
| ☐ **g** Suggest a time and place. | Say hello. Say who you are and why you are phoning. **o** 2 |
| ☐ **h** Tell Jim you have a suggestion. | |

**Your turn** **B** Work in pairs: Astrid and Jim. Use the steps in exercise A in the correct order to have a similar conversation.

**A:** *Astrid Schmidt.*

**B:** *Hello, Astrid. It's Jim. You asked me to call you.*

## Writing

**A** Complete the report with the correct forms of the verbs in brackets.

---

### Special Report

**From** Astrid Schmidt
**To** Carmen Paredes

## Supersport in the US

Supersport ¹ <u>lost</u> (lose) money in the US last year; now we ² <u>are making</u> a profit.

We ³ _____ (have) problems with our stock at first, but now the computer system ⁴ _____ _____ (work) well.

We ⁵ _____ (ask) the computer manager ⁶ _____ _____ (go) to Sacramento to train staff.

I ⁷ _____ (be) very happy with the situation now. But I ⁸ _____ (advise) you ⁹ _____ _____ (think) very hard before you open stores in other new markets.

If you need more information, please let me know.

---

## Checklist

✓ **advise, want, tell:** Astrid wants the computer systems manager to phone her.

✓ **agree, disagree:** Harry disagreed with Astrid.

✓ **expressions:** *If you need more information, please let me know.*

# Review 19–24

**A** Newspaper headlines often use the present simple instead of the present perfect. Change the headlines into normal English, using the present perfect. Add extra words where necessary.

**1**
> **Supersport buys Mexican store chain for €1 billion**

*Supersport has bought a Mexican store chain for €1 billion.*

**2**
> **30,000 people find jobs this month**

**3**
> **Australian dollar rises to €1.25**

**4**
> **20-year-old pilot flies alone round world in small plane**

**5**
> **BRAZIL BEATS ENGLAND 2–1**

**6**
> **Man wins €10 million at Monte Carlo casino**

**7**
> **Disney announces new park in Spain**

**B** Match the two parts of the sentences in the most logical way.

I went to the ...

1 supermarket, but they didn't have any
2 bank, but they didn't want to give me any
3 travel agent, but they couldn't give me any
4 job centre, but I couldn't find any
5 sports shop, but they didn't have any
6 flat agency, but they didn't have any
7 garage, but they didn't have any
8 language, school but they don't offer any

a money.
b information about holidays in Cuba.
c fruit.
d skis in stock.
e work.
f petrol.
g courses in Chinese.
h flats under €1,500 a month.

**C** Look at this range of cars and write *T* (true) or *F* (false).

| | Texas | Utah | Virginia | Wisconsin |
|---|---|---|---|---|
| **price** | $16,700 | $22,200 | $25,000 | $19,500 |
| **world sales last year** | 533,000 | 244,000 | 183,000 | 122,000 |
| **profit per car sold** | $870 | $1,500 | $2,200 | $2,100 |

1 The range starts at $19,500. __F__
2 The Utah and the Wisconsin are mid-priced. _____
3 The most expensive car is the Virginia. _____
4 The Wisconsin is cheaper than the Utah. _____
5 The cheapest car is the Texas. _____
6 If the Texas offers more than other cars at the same price, it is good value for money. _____
7 Sales of the Utah were higher than sales of the Virginia. _____
8 Sales of the Texas were highest. _____
9 When you look at profit per car sold, the Texas was more profitable than the Virginia. _____
10 The most profitable car was the Virginia. _____

**D** Write out the figures for the prices and the sales of the cars in exercise C.

*The Texas costs sixteen thousand seven hundred dollars. World sales last year were five hundred and thirty-three thousand.*

**E** Complete the sentences, using the verbs in the box.

| do | go | listen | pay | see | ~~walk~~ |
|---|---|---|---|---|---|

1 We've missed the last bus, so we must _walk_.
2 You must _____ when I'm speaking.
3 I must _____ now – my taxi's waiting outside.
4 I'm ill. I must go and _____ a doctor.
5 We've finished eating. Now we must _____ the bill.
6 Her assistant is on holiday. She must _____ everything herself.

**F** Complete the crossword.

**Across**
3 If you don't make a loss, you make a ... (6)
7 when you ask people what they think of your products (6, 8)
8 the help that you get in a shop (7)
9 when a company does not make a profit (4)
10 the money you get from the products you sell (5)

**Down**
1 the companies in the same market as you (11)
2 shops (6)
4 numbers (7)
5 something that you sell (7)
6 a group of products (5)

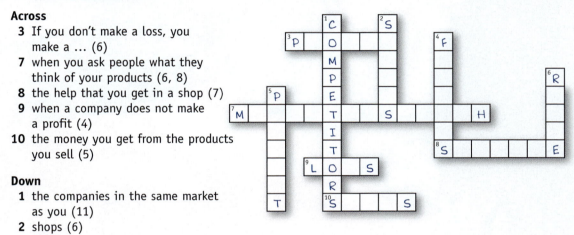

**G** Correct the sentences. There is one mistake in each sentence.

1 I want ~~that you~~ *you to* help me with this job.
2 I am agree with you about this problem.
3 She told to me to leave.
4 I advised him that he sees a doctor.
5 She wanted that we change the way we work.
6 We were disagreed with her.

**H** You have arranged a meeting with Astrid Schmidt in New York for next Wednesday, but you want to change the arrangements. Write sentences for your e-mail to Astrid.

1 Say you can't come to New York on Wednesday – meeting in Paris on same day
*Unfortunately I can't come to New York on Wednesday. I have a meeting in Paris on the same day.*
2 Suggest Tuesday next week, at 12 noon, instead. *How about ...*
3 Apologise for the change. *I'm sorry about ...*
4 Say you are looking forward to the meeting. *I'm looking forward to ...*
5 End your e-mail. *Best ...*

**I** Use some of the words and expressions from Units 19–24 to talk or write about yourself or the characters and situations.

*We had sales of $10 million last year and profits of $1 million.*

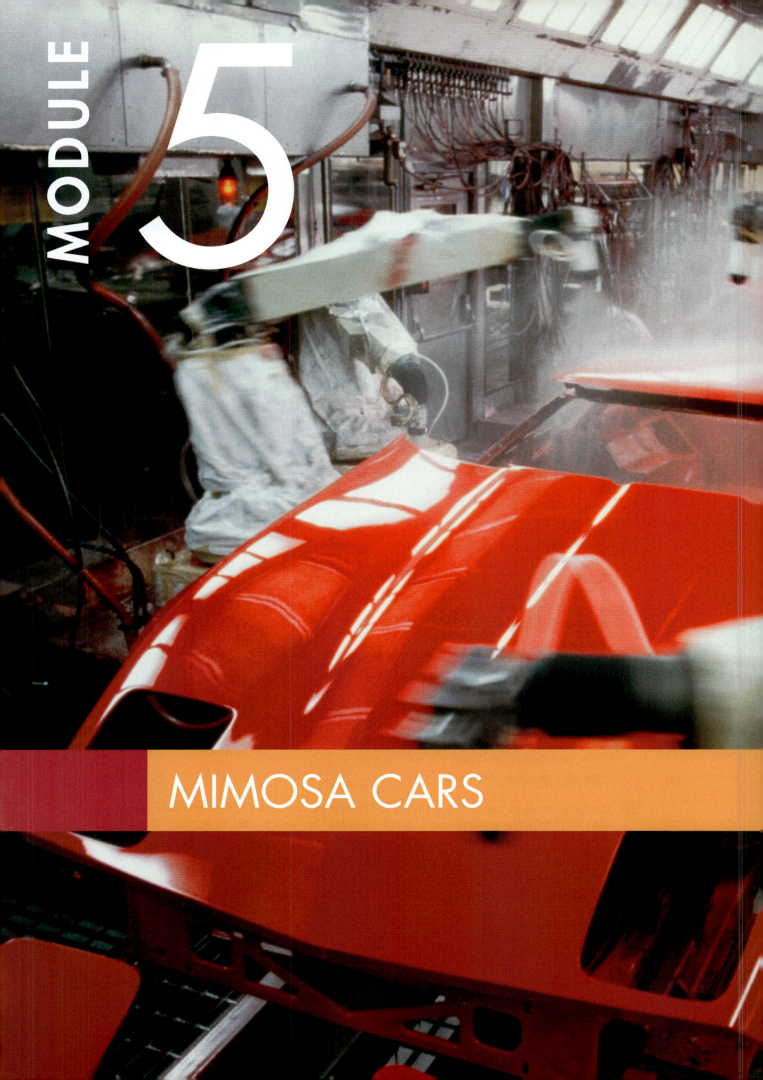

# MIMOSA CARS

The Malaysian group KL Industries buys Mimosa Cars, an Italian sports car company. KLI want to invest in Mimosa and produce new models. Mimosa's production manager, Paolo Ponte, goes to Malaysia to meet Saleem Bashir of KLI.

# 25 Don't drive too fast!

**Reading** **A** Read the article.

WORLD SPORTS CAR NEWS

## HAPPY BIRTHDAY, Mimosa GLX

### RAY BAXTER REPORTS FROM MODENA

Like Alfa Romeo, Bugatti and Maserati, Mimosa is one of the great names in Italian sports cars. The Mimosa GLX model is 20 years old this week. I've had one for 15 years, and I love it. With a top speed of 220 kilometres per hour, it's one of the best ways of getting from A to B in style. It has two seats and space for a very small bag at the back.

Mimosa grew rapidly in the 1980s. In the 1990s, its sales fell rapidly year by year. The GLX design is showing its age. It has new and more powerful competitors.

**B** Now write *T* (true) or *F* (false).

1 Mimosa is an Italian car. ___T___

2 The GLX model is 15 years old. _____

3 Ray Baxter has had a GLX for 15 years. _____

4 The car has seats for four passengers. _____

5 The GLX is getting old. _____

6 It is more powerful than its competitors. _____

## Grammar  adverbs

*Mimosa grew **rapidly** in the 1980s.*

You can use an adverb to tell you more about a verb.

**A** **Complete the table.**

|  | adjective | adverb |
|---|---|---|
| **standard adjective** | quick    slow | quickly    _____ |
| **adjective ends in -y** | easy    happy | easily    _____ |
| **adverb same as adjective** | early    late    fast    hard | early    _____    _____    _____ |
| **irregular** | good | well |

**B** **Complete the sentences with the adverb forms of the adjectives in brackets.**

1 The GLX is a powerful car. You can _easily_ do more than 200 kilometres per hour. Don't drive too _fast_ ! (easy, fast)

2 But sales are falling _____ . Mimosa is _____ in a bad situation. (rapid, clear)

3 At Mimosa, employees must get to the office _____ , work _____ and stay _____ every evening. (early, hard, late)

4 People like working for Mimosa. They _____ work until 9 every evening. (happy)

5 In this company, the designers _____ wear jeans, not business suits. (usual)

■ More information:
Grammar overview
page 113

▶ More practice:
Workbook page 58

## ON THE LINE

**A** 🔊 25.1 **Melanie Taylor is a senior designer at Mimosa Cars. Listen to the four messages on her voice-mail. Find the reasons for the phone calls and the numbers for Melanie to call.**

|  | reason | number to call |
|---|---|---|
| **1** Jong-Hun Park | He's visiting Modena on Tuesday. He wants to meet Melanie for lunch. | 00 33 1 78 32 45 61 |
| **2** Ray Baxter | | |
| **3** Barbara Strauss | | |
| **4** Alessandra Tivoli | | |

**Your turn** **B** **Work in pairs. Student A looks at this page. Student B looks at page 159.**

**Student A**

- You are Melanie Taylor. Phone Alessandra Tivoli (Student B) and ask her what the secret is. *Hi, Alessandra. I got your message. What's the secret?*
- Ask her how she knows this.
- Ask her the name of the company.
- Ask if they are going to put money into Mimosa.
- End the conversation.

## Checklist

✓ adverbs: *Mimosa grew rapidly in the 1980s.*

✓ voice-mail messages: *This is Barbara Strauss at Autostudio in Hamburg.*

✓ call someone back: *I got your message.*

# 26 KLI are going to buy Mimosa

## Vocabulary

**A** Complete the chart, using the job titles in the box.

> chairman/chairwoman/chairperson – the most important person in the company
>
> chief executive or chief executive officer (CEO) – the most important manager. This person sometimes also has the job of chairman/chairwoman.
>
> chief financial officer
> head of production
> chief designer
> marketing director

### Mimosa Cars
#### BOARD OF DIRECTORS

**Silvio Berio,** [1] chairman
and [2] _____ _____

| 3 _____ _____ _____ (manages company money) | 4 _____ _____ _____ (manages the car factory) | 5 _____ _____ (manages the designers) | 6 _____ _____ (manages marketing) |
|---|---|---|---|

## Listening

**A** Silvio Berio, chairman and chief executive officer of Mimosa Cars, holds a press conference. Listen and answer the questions.

1 How many people do you hear?
2 Who are they?
3 What is the important announcement – a, b or c?
   a Mimosa are going to stop making cars.
   b KL Industries are going to buy Mimosa.
   c Silvio Berio is going to leave Mimosa.

## Grammar  future with *going to*

You can use *going to* and the base form of the verb to talk about plans and intentions.
*What are KLI **going to** do? – They're **going to** buy Mimosa Cars.*

**A** You are interviewing Johnny Choo, chairman of KL Industries. Complete the questions and answers.

1 What <u>are</u> <u>you</u> <u>going</u> <u>to</u> do with Mimosa?
   – We<u>'re</u> <u>going</u> <u>to</u> invest a lot of money in the company.

2 How much ____ ____ ____ ____ invest?
   – We____ ____ ____ spend 500 million euros over the next five years.

3 What ____ ____ ____ ____ spend the money on?
   – I____ ____ ____ replace the older models like the GLX and introduce some new models.

4 How ____ ____ ____ ____ develop the engineering side?
   – KL Industries ____ ____ ____ give Mimosa a lot of technical help.

■ More information:
Grammar overview
page 108

**B** 🔘 *26.2* Now listen, check and repeat.

**C** Practise reading the conversation in pairs.

## ON THE LINE

**A** 🔘 *26.3* After KLI buy Mimosa, Johnny Choo stays in Italy for a month. He has an office at Mimosa's headquarters in Modena. He gets a lot of phone calls. His personal assistant answers the phone.
Listen to three calls. Who calls? Does Johnny talk to the person in each call?

**B** Listen to the conversations again and tick the conversation in which you hear each expression.

| conversation | 1 | 2 | 3 |
|---|---|---|---|
| *May I ask who's calling?* | ✓ | ✓ | ✓ |
| *I'm putting you through.* | ✓ | | |
| *Mr Choo isn't available.* | | | |
| *He's in a meeting.* | | | |
| *Mr Choo isn't in his office.* | | | |
| *Please could you call …* | | | |

**Your turn**

**C** Work in pairs. Student A looks at this page.
Student B looks at page 159.

**Student A**

You are Johnny Choo's PA. You receive three calls. Find out who is calling and what their job is. You don't put through calls 1 and 2 – explain why to the caller – but you do put through call 3. Complete the table.

| | name of caller | job | put him/her through? | reason |
|---|---|---|---|---|
| 1 | Gudrun Olafsson | journalist at Sports Car Gazette | no | all journalists must call the PR firm in Milan |
| 2 | | | no | in a meeting |
| 3 | | | yes | |

## Checklist

✓ job titles:
chief executive officer, head
of production …

✓ future with *going to*: We're
going to spend 500 million
euros.

✓ call handling: *I'm putting you
through. / Mr Choo isn't
available.*

# 27 Have you ever been to Malaysia?

**Reading** **A** Saleem Bashir is an engineer at KL Industries in Kuala Lumpur. He has been to see Paolo Ponte, head of production at Mimosa Cars in Modena. Read the e-mail that he wrote after his visit.

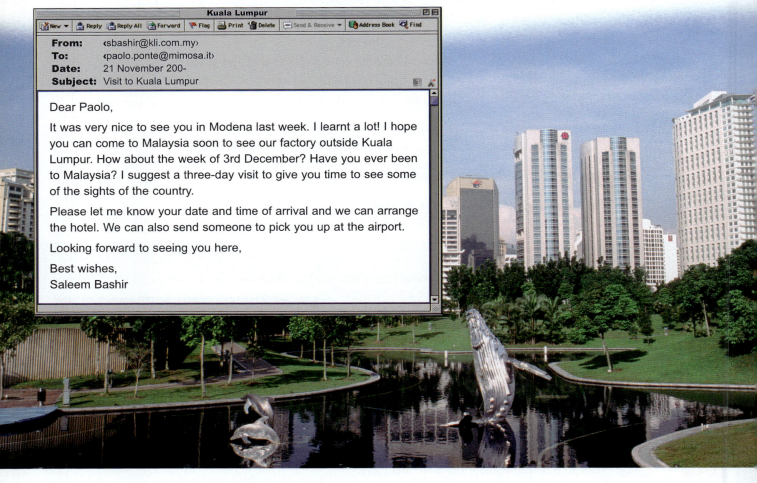

**Kuala Lumpur**

New | Reply | Reply All | Forward | Flag | Print | Delete | Send & Receive | Address Book | Find

From: ‹sbashir@kli.com.my›
To: ‹paolo.ponte@mimosa.it›
Date: 21 November 200-
Subject: Visit to Kuala Lumpur

Dear Paolo,

It was very nice to see you in Modena last week. I learnt a lot! I hope you can come to Malaysia soon to see our factory outside Kuala Lumpur. How about the week of 3rd December? Have you ever been to Malaysia? I suggest a three-day visit to give you time to see some of the sights of the country.

Please let me know your date and time of arrival and we can arrange the hotel. We can also send someone to pick you up at the airport.

Looking forward to seeing you here,

Best wishes,
Saleem Bashir

**B** Now answer the questions.

1 When was Saleem Bashir in Modena?  *Last week.*
2 Was the trip useful?
3 What is the purpose of his e-mail to Paolo Ponte?

4 What does Saleem want to show Paolo?
5 How many days does Saleem suggest for the visit?
6 Is Saleem going to meet Paolo at the airport?

**Grammar** **present perfect with *ever* and *never***

You can use the present perfect with *ever* and *never* to talk about experiences.

You can ask questions with *ever*.
*Have you ever been to Malaysia?*

You can answer like this:
*No. I've never been to Malaysia, but I've been to Singapore.*

**A** Work in pairs. Ask and answer questions about these places.

1 Washington ✗ / New York ✓

A: *Have you ever been to Washington?*
B: *No, I've never been to Washington, but I've been to New York.*

2 Sweden ✗ / Norway ✓
3 Venice ✗ / Rome ✓
4 Egypt ✗ / Tunisia ✓
5 Johannesburg ✗ / Cape Town ✓

▶ More practice:
Workbook page 62

## Writing

**A** Complete Paolo Ponte's reply to Saleem's e-mail on page 74. Use the correct forms of the verbs in brackets.

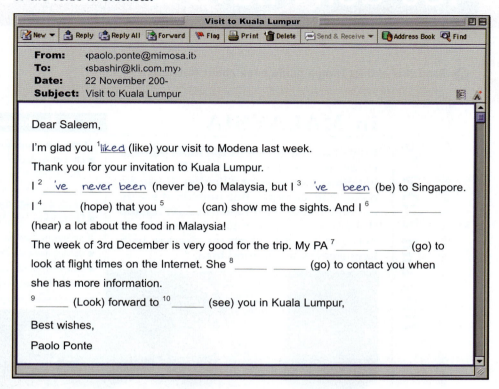

Visit to Kuala Lumpur

New ▾ | Reply | Reply All | Forward | Flag | Print | Delete | Send & Receive ▾ | Address Book | Find

From: ‹paolo.ponte@mimosa.it›
To: ‹sbashir@kli.com.my›
Date: 22 November 200-
Subject: Visit to Kuala Lumpur

Dear Saleem,

I'm glad you [1] liked (like) your visit to Modena last week.

Thank you for your invitation to Kuala Lumpur.

I [2] 've never been (never be) to Malaysia, but I [3] 've been (be) to Singapore.

I [4] _____ (hope) that you [5] _____ (can) show me the sights. And I [6] _____ _____ (hear) a lot about the food in Malaysia!

The week of 3rd December is very good for the trip. My PA [7] _____ _____ (go) to look at flight times on the Internet. She [8] _____ _____ (go) to contact you when she has more information.

[9] _____ (Look) forward to [10] _____ (see) you in Kuala Lumpur,

Best wishes,

Paolo Ponte

## Listening and speaking

**A** 🔵 27.1 Paolo Ponte is talking to Melanie Taylor in the company restaurant about his trip to Malaysia. Work in pairs. Student A looks at this page. Student B looks at page 159.

**Student A**

You are Melanie Taylor. Listen to the beginning of your conversation with Paolo (Student B). Then continue the conversation. Ask:

- when he is leaving.
- how he is getting there.
- where he is changing planes.
- when he is arriving.
- how long he is going for.
- where he is staying.

◀ Your turn ▶ **B** Plan a trip and make notes about it: where you are going, when you are leaving, how you are getting there, etc.

*Where are you going?*

**C** Now work in pairs. Ask your partner about their trip, using the questions you wrote in exercise B.

**A:** *Where are you going?*
**B:** *To ...*
**A:** *When are you leaving?*
**B:** *On Monday afternoon.*

**D** Talk about your partner's trip. ... *is going to ...*

## Checklist

✓ use the present perfect with *ever* and *never* to talk about experiences: *Have you ever been to Washington? – No, I've never been to Washington, but I've been to New York.*

✓ expressions: *Please let me know your date and time of arrival.*

# 28 You don't have to wear a jacket

**Reading and grammar 1**

**A** Read this extract from a guide book about Malaysia.

**DOs and DON'Ts**

## in MALAYSIA

Kuala Lumpur is one of the most modern cities in south-east Asia. Most new buildings have air-conditioning. It can be quite cold indoors! But outside it's very hot and humid. To do business, shirts and ties are necessary for men, but a jacket is not. For women, shirts or dresses with long sleeves are a good idea.

### As in the rest of Malaysia

There are some basic rules:

■ Do not shake someone's hand unless they offer it first.
■ Do not touch people's heads, even the heads of children.
■ Do not kiss in public.

If someone invites you to their home:

■ do not wear shorts.
■ take a small gift like flowers or fruit.
■ take off your shoes when entering.
■ do not start eating before you are invited to.

*must/mustn't; don't have to*

*You **must** wear a tie, but you **don't have to** wear a jacket.*
*You **mustn't** wear shorts.*

**B** Make one sentence about the extract using *mustn't* and one using *don't have to*.

You mustn't touch people's heads.     You don't have to wear a jacket.

**C** Complete the advice about visiting a particular country, using *mustn't* or *don't have to*.

You ...

1 <u>don't have to</u> speak the language – everyone speaks English. But they like it if you know one or two words of their language.
2 _____ keep your shoes on when you visit someone. People always take their shoes off.
3 _____ take a gift like flowers when someone invites you to dinner, but it's probably a good idea.
4 _____ start eating before other people at a barbecue or dinner party.
5 _____ phone the person the next day to say thank you. But they like it if you do phone.

■ More information: Grammar overview pages 108–109

**D** Which country do you think this advice is for?

**a** Italy    **b** Sweden    **c** Russia

**Your turn** > **E** Give advice for visitors to your country.

Think about:

• gifts    • food    • how to dress

*If you visit someone in my country, you must take a small gift.*

▶ More practice: Workbook page 64

## Grammar 2 · *how much* with uncountable nouns

*How much* work did they do?

Some nouns are uncountable – they have no plural. Here are some of them:

*advice, information, time, help, money, work.*

You ask questions with *How much* ... (not *How many* ...).

**A:** *How much money are you going to take?*

**B:** *Not much. KLI are going to pay for everything.*

**A** **Melanie Taylor is talking to Paolo Ponte about his trip to Malaysia.
Match Melanie's questions to Paolo's answers.**

How much ...

1 free time are you going to get?

2 work are you going to do when you're there?

3 help are you going to get when you arrive?

4 information do you have about the country?

5 money are you taking?

a A lot. This is a work trip, not a holiday!

b I'm free on Saturday, I think.

c I've read three guide books.

d Not much. But I'm taking my credit cards with me.

e Saleem's driver is meeting me at the airport.

■ More information:
Grammar overview
page 112

## ON THE LINE

**A** **28.1 Paolo Ponte arrives in Kuala Lumpur. He phones Saleem Bashir. Listen to the conversation and answer the questions.**

1 Where is Paolo Ponte?  *He's at Kuala Lumpur airport.*

2 Did Paolo send Saleem an e-mail about his arrival time?

3 Who told Saleem's driver about this change?

4 Why isn't Saleem's driver at the airport to meet Paolo?

5 Where is his driver now?

6 Where are Saleem and Paolo going to meet?

**Your turn**

**B** **Work in pairs.
Student A looks at this page.
Student B looks at page 159.**

**Student A**

• You arrive in Sydney after a 15-hour flight to visit a friend there. Your flight arrives at 7 am. Your friend (Student B) isn't at the airport to meet you, as promised. Phone on your mobile to find out why.

*Hi, ... It's ... I'm at Sydney airport.*

• End the conversation.

## Checklist

✓ must/mustn't; *don't have to: You don't have to wear a jacket.*

✓ *how much* with uncountable nouns: *How much money are you going to take? – Not much.*

✓ deal with mix-ups on the phone: *There's been a mix-up.*

# 29 Welcome to the hotel

**Reading and vocabulary**

**A** Read the hotel guide.

## Welcome to the
## Hotel Shangrila
## Kuala Lumpur

*Dear Guest,*

All guest rooms are equipped with a range of facilities: direct-dial telephone, 24-hour room service, colour TV with a special movie channel (6 pm to 2 am), controls for lights and air-conditioning, minibar and tea and coffee-making facilities. All rooms have a personal safe.

Your room is on the 17th floor. The Penang Lounge on the 19th floor serves breakfast from 7 to 10.30 am. The bar in this lounge is open from 6.30 to 11 pm.

Take the high-speed lift to the Shangrila Restaurant on the 51st floor, with a wide range of Asian and European dishes. All restaurant dishes are available in your room, of course. Just dial 129 for room service.

And there's the Power Gym Club and Pool with all sports facilities. Open from 8 am to 11 pm.

When you leave, you can check out very fast – in less than one minute.

If you need more information, just pick up the phone and call reception by dialling 0.

*Have a nice stay!*

**B** Now match the hotel words to their meanings.

1 reception      **a** places, equipment, etc for a particular purpose

2 room service      **b** a room where you can read, talk, etc

3 safe      **c** the first place you go when you arrive

4 lounge      **d** when people bring things to your room

5 facilities      **e** machine that takes you to another floor – called an 'elevator' in American English

6 lift      **f** a strong metal box for valuable things

**C** Now answer the questions.

Where do you go if you want to:

1 have breakfast?    *The Penang Lounge.*

2 eat Chinese food?

3 go for a swim?

When can you:

4 watch a film on TV?

5 have breakfast in the lounge?

6 get something to eat in your room?

## Grammar

### verbs + prepositions

Some verbs are used with prepositions.
*Just **pick up** the phone and call reception.*

Sometimes the meaning of a verb changes when it is used with a preposition. Compare these sentences.
*Please can you **check** these figures for me?*
*At this hotel, you can **check out** very quickly.*

**Ⓐ Complete the sentences, using the prepositions in the box.**

| ~~up~~ | on | out | down | ~~in~~ | up | up | out | up | in |
|---|---|---|---|---|---|---|---|---|---|

1 Check __in__ at reception.
2 Go __up__ to the 19th floor and go into your room.
3 Turn _____ the lights.
4 Put your money _____ the safe.
5 Take a drink _____ of the minibar.
6 The air-conditioning is on: if you're hot, turn it _____ .

7 Go to sleep and wake _____ .
8 Pick _____ the phone and order breakfast.
9 From the 19th floor, take the lift _____ to reception.
10 Check _____ of the hotel.

- More information: Grammar overview page 110
▶ More practice: Workbook page 67

**Ⓑ 29.1 Now listen, check and repeat.**

## Listening and speaking

**Ⓐ 29.2 Listen to the conversation between Saleem and Paolo when they meet at the hotel. Write *T* (true) or *F* (false).**

1 Paolo was tired after his flight, so he slept for a couple of hours. __T__
2 The air-conditioning in his room is broken. _____
3 Paolo says that his colleagues at Mimosa are excited about the new situation. _____
4 Saleem says it will be easy and quick to develop Mimosa. _____
5 Saleem says that Paolo is going to visit the factory outside Kuala Lumpur tomorrow. _____
6 Paolo does not want to see the factory. _____
7 Saleem suggests that they continue to work on Saturday. _____

**◀ Your turn ▶**

**Ⓑ Work in pairs. Ask and answer questions about a recent business trip or holiday.**

1 Where did you go? Was it a business trip or a holiday?   *I went to Lagos on business.*
2 Was it hot or cold?
3 Did you take the right clothes?
4 Who did you see?
5 Which places did you visit?
6 How long did you stay?
7 Did you enjoy your trip?

## Writing

**Ⓐ Paolo has now returned to Italy after his trip. Write sentences for Paolo's e-mail to Saleem, thanking him.**

1 thank him for a pleasant stay   *Thank you for such a pleasant stay in Malaysia.*
2 flights back very smooth – no delays   *The flights back to Italy were very smooth. There were no delays.*
3 visit to the KLI factory – very interesting
4 enjoyed the trip to the coast on Saturday – good to see something of Malaysia
5 look forward to working with him on the GLX mark 2

## Checklist

✓ hotel vocabulary: *reception, room service, lounge …*

✓ verbs + prepositions: *check in, wake up*

✓ expressions: *Thank you for such a pleasant stay.*

# 30 It will be a big success

## Reading

**A** Read the press release.

Press release

### Mimosa announce GLX mark 2

We are pleased to announce a new model to replace the classic GLX mark 1, designed more than 20 years ago. Thanks to investment from the Malaysian company KL Industries, Mimosa are planning to produce the GLX mark 2. KLI have said that they will put 500 million euros into Mimosa over the next five years. The GLX mark 2 is one of three models that Mimosa will produce.

'The GLX mark 2 will be the most advanced sports car in the world,' says Silvio Berio, chief executive of Mimosa. 'We'll launch the car at the Paris Motor Show next year. Plans for production and marketing are going very well. We're right on schedule. The new GLX will be a big success, I'm sure.'

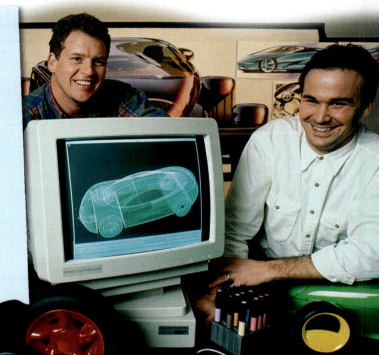

**B** Now circle the correct words to complete each sentence.

**1** The GLX mark 1 is more than ...
  **a** 10 years old.   **b** 15 years old.   **c** 20 years old.

**2** The amount KLI will invest in Mimosa over the next five years is ...
  **a** 300 million euros.   **b** 500 million euros.   **c** 700 million euros.

**3** The GLX mark 2 is ... that Mimosa will produce.
  **a** the only new model.   **b** one of two models.   **c** one of three models.

**4** The GLX mark 2 will be the most modern sports car in ...
  **a** the world.   **b** the United States.   **c** Europe.

**5** Mimosa will launch the car in ...
  **a** Frankfurt.   **b** Paris.   **c** New York.

**6** Plans for the GLX are ...
  **a** on schedule.   **b** behind schedule.   **c** ahead of schedule.

## Grammar

### future with *will*

You can use the future simple talk about:

- future events.

    *We'll launch the car at the Paris Motor Show next year.*

- a decision you make at the time of speaking.

    *I'll e-mail you the schedule later today.*

You make the future simple with *will* or *will not* and the base form of the verb. In spoken English, you often use the short forms *'ll* and *won't*.

**A** Complete the sentences, using the future simple.
Then add *1* (future event) or *2* (decision at the time of speaking).

1 Our sales ___will___ increase by 200 per cent next year. ___1___
2 I'_____ give you a call this afternoon. _____
3 The company _____ start production of the new model next month. _____
4 The new model _____ be a big success. _____
5 I'm staying at home. I _____ go to the meeting after all. _____

■ More information:
Grammar overview
page 108

## Vocabulary and listening

**A** Complete the text, using the words and expressions in the box.

| behind schedule    complete    on schedule    project    schedule    stage |

A particular piece of work is a ¹project . A project is made up of different ²_____s. You can do some stages at the same time but you can only do other stages when the earlier stage is ³_____ .The ⁴_____ gives the times for the different stages of the project. If you finish a project on time, you finish it ⁵_____ _____ . If you finish it late, you finish ⁶_____ _____ .

**B** 🔵 **30.1** Paolo Ponte, Melanie Taylor and Adriana Cardinale are having a meeting at Mimosa Cars. Listen and tick all the words/expressions you hear from the box in exercise A.

## Writing

**A** Paolo Ponte writes a memo to the chief executive of Mimosa about the design, advertising and production of the GLX mark 2. Complete the memo with the correct forms of the verbs in brackets.

# Memo

| From: | Paolo Ponte |
| To: | Silvio Berio |
| Date: | 7 January |

This ¹_is_ (be) to confirm the details of a meeting I ²_had_ (have) yesterday with Melanie Taylor, a senior designer in the design department, and Adriana Cardinale, head of marketing.

The design stage for the GLX mark 2 ³_____ _____ (go) well and we ⁴_____ _____ (complete) it in June.

Adriana ⁵_____ _____ (look) for advertising agencies, and the advertising ⁶_____ _____ (start) in September next year, just before the Paris Motor Show.

I ⁷_____ (be) sure we ⁸_____ _____ (finish) the project on schedule, and the new GLX ⁹_____ _____ (be) a big success.

Best regards,
Paolo Ponte

## Checklist

✔future with *will*: *The GLX will be a big success.*    ✔schedules: *I hope we don't get behind schedule.*    ✔expressions: *This is to confirm ...*

# Review 25–30

**A** Complete the sentences with the correct words.

1 Don't talk so _fast_ (fast/fastly). I can't follow.

2 I _____ (usual/usually) go on holiday in August.

3 I'm a morning person. I _____ (happy/happily) start work at 6 am.

4 Think _____ (careful/carefully) about the question before you answer it.

5 Your spelling is _____ (terrible/terribly). Don't be so _____ (careless/carelessly).

6 This job is simple. You can _____ (easy/easily) do it in half an hour.

7 This machine is _____ (dangerous/dangerously). Don't be _____ (careless/carelessly) when you use it.

**B** Match the directors to the things they typically do.

1 chairwoman and chief executive

2 head of production

3 chief financial officer

4 chief designer

5 marketing director

a manages workers in the factory

b asks banks for more money

c gives journalists very important news about the company

d chooses an advertising agency

e tells a designer to make drawings of a new product

**C** These sentences are about a company in difficulty.
Circle the words that show what is probably going to happen.

1 The company's sales are falling fast. It's going to …
  a make a big profit.        **b** lose a lot of money.

2 The other directors don't like the chief executive. They're going to ask him to …
  a leave the board of directors.        b stay in his job.

3 The sales reps haven't sold enough. The sales director is going to …
  a get bigger cars for them.        b tell them to sell more.

4 The marketing director isn't happy with the advertising agency. She's going to …
  a find another one.        b increase what she spends with the agency.

5 The designers have produced no new designs for a year. They're going to …
  a lose their jobs.        b get a pay increase.

6 The chief financial officer is very unhappy about the financial situation. She's going to …
  a ask the banks to lend more money.    b buy another company.

**D** Work in pairs. Ask and answer questions, using the present perfect.

1 read / a book by John Grisham
  **A:** *Have you ever read a book by John Grisham?*
  **B:** *No, I haven't. / Yes, I have. I've read 'The Partner'. It's very exciting.*

2 see / a film with Nicole Kidman

3 drive / a very fast car

4 ride / a motorbike

5 drink / Australian wine

6 eat / caviar

**E** Complete the advice about working at Serioco, using *must*, *mustn't* or *don't have to*.

## Serioco

**HOUSE RULES**

On Mondays to Thursdays you ¹<u>must</u> dress formally. Men ²_____ wear business suits. Women ³_____ wear trouser suits: skirts are obligatory. However, on Fridays, you can dress more informally: you ⁴_____ wear a business suit if you don't want to. But you ⁵_____ wear jeans: they are not allowed at any time.

When speaking to colleagues, you ⁶_____ use family names: the use of first names is not permitted.

You ⁷_____ do all work in the company's offices. You ⁸_____ take work home.

**F** Complete the sentences, using the words in the box.

| up | in | down | up | ~~on~~ | up | out | up | ~~off~~ | up |

1 When you want to watch television, you turn it <u>on</u> . When you've finished, you turn it <u>off</u> .
2 If the sound from a radio, television, etc is too loud, you turn it _____ . If it isn't loud enough, you turn it _____ .
3 When you arrive at a hotel or at an airport for a flight, you check _____ . When you leave a hotel, you check _____ .
4 When someone stops sleeping, they wake _____ . When someone leaves their bed, they get _____ .
5 When you want to make a phone call, you pick _____ the telephone.
6 If you don't want to use the stairs to the 19th floor, you can go _____ in the lift.

**G** Complete the crossword.

**Across**
1 If you want to eat in your room, phone for room ... (7)
3 the American English word for 4 down (8)
5 The hotel has very good ... for sport and swimming. (10)
6 If you want to read a newspaper, go to the ... (6)

**Down**
1 Put valuable items in the ... (4)
2 If you want more information about the hotel, just phone ... (9)
4 Don't take the stairs – use the ... (4)

Crossword grid: 1 Across SERVICE, 3 Across E...E...R, 5 Across F...I...S, 6 Across L...N...T, 4 Down L

**H** Match the sentences on the left to the responses on the right.

1 These bags are heavy.
2 I don't know when the meeting starts.
3 We can eat in an hour.
4 We can always drive down to Spain.
5 I'm going to her house but I don't have a map.
6 I've borrowed John's chair.
7 They've left the country. They say they'll never come back.

a You won't find it without one.
b You'll see – they'll be back in six months.
c The plane will be quicker.
d The children won't be hungry.
e I'll phone and find out.
f I'll carry them for you.
g Don't worry – he won't mind.

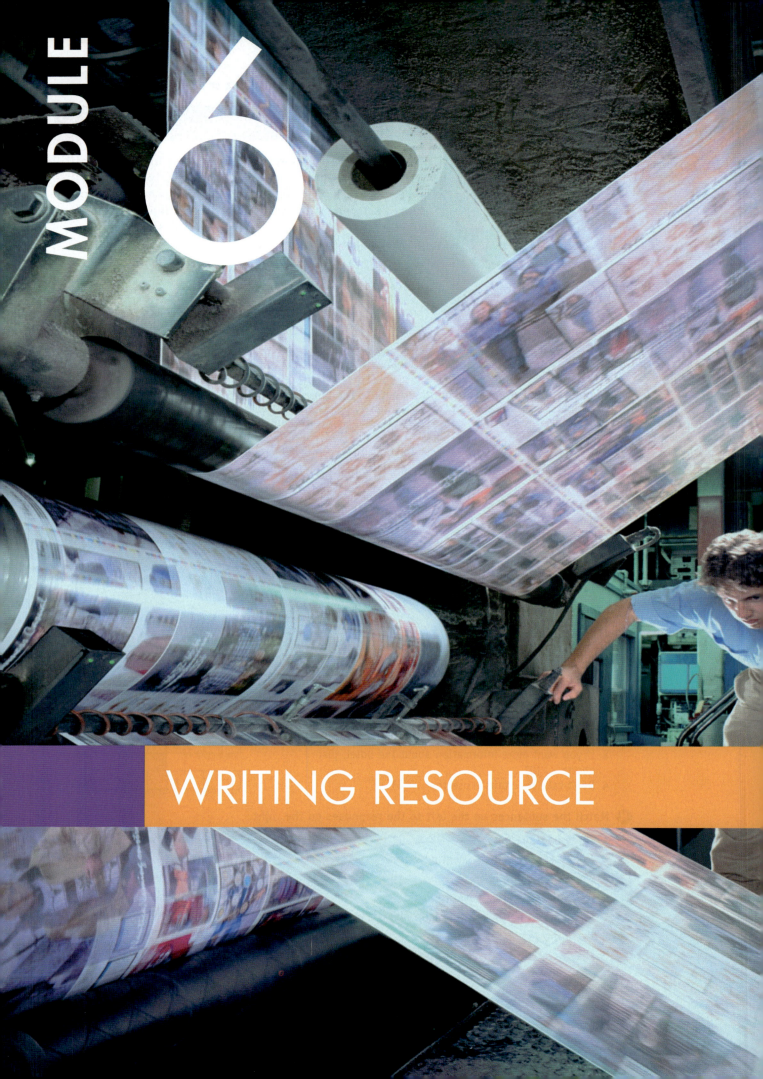

MODULE

6

WRITING RESOURCE

This module gives further practice in writing letters, faxes, e-mails and short reports. Canapub, a Canadian publishing multinational, launches a women's magazine in Latin America. Market research shows that sales will be good, and Canapub's Charlotte Ramsden recruits a marketing manager, Luisa Barcarem, to take care of the launch. Sales are even better than expected.

**Fax** **A** Read this fax from Charlotte Ramsden, chief editor of *Novina* in Toronto, to Francisco Solano, head of a market research firm in Buenos Aires.

## Canapub Inc

550 Bloor Street, Toronto, ON, Canada
Tel +1 416 213 8480, Fax +1 416 213 8495

FAX

| | |
|---|---|
| Date | 10 January 200- |
| Fax no. | +54 11 4343 5032 |
| No. of pages incl. this one | 2 |

| From | Charlotte Ramsden |
|---|---|
| To | AMR, Buenos Aires |
| Attn | Francisco Solano |

Dear Francisco,

It was good seeing you in Toronto yesterday. I hope you had a good trip back to Buenos Aires.

Following our discussions, this is to confirm that we would like you to do market research into the possibility of a Spanish-language edition of *Novina* for Latin America. We would like you to do research in all the main Spanish-speaking countries.

Before we launch this edition, we need to know 1) how many people will buy the magazine, 2) the maximum price they will pay for it, and 3) what they are most interested in reading about.

Please let me know how long this research will take and how much you will charge.

Looking forward to hearing from you,

Best wishes,

*Charlotte Ramsden*

Charlotte Ramsden
Chief Editor, *Novina*

**B** You are Francisco Solano. Complete his reply fax to Charlotte Ramsden. Put the verbs in brackets in the correct form and add other words as necessary.

**FAX**

Thank you ¹ _for_ a very useful meeting yesterday. I ² _had_ (have) a very good trip back here – no problems at all.

I ³ _____ _____ (send) you our standard contract by FedEx courier. Please could ⁴_____ ⁵_____ (sign) ⁶_____ ⁷_____ (return) ⁸_____ as soon as possible. The research ⁹_____ _____ (take) two months. The cost ¹⁰_____ _____ (be) US$ 50,000: 25,000 on signature of contract ¹¹_____ 25,000 on completion.

If you have any questions, please do ¹²_____ hesitate ¹³_____ contact me.

Best regards,

*Francisco Solano*

Francisco Solano
Head of Research

**C** Imagine that a possible supplier comes to see a manager in your organisation to discuss the supply of a particular service. Write a fax from the manager to the supplier to confirm what they discussed and decided.

The service might be, for example:
- a market research report
- advertising in the local phone book
- a loan

**Company description**

**A** Read the extract from a trade magazine about *Novina*. Then read the description of *Novina* based on the extract.

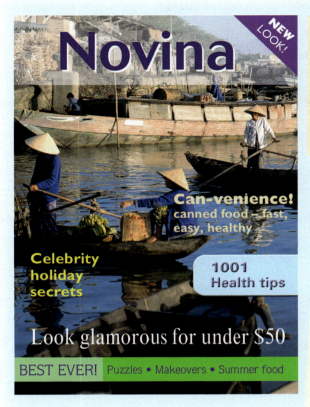

**NOVINA**

**Publishers** Canapub Inc., international Canadian company, Toronto
**Offices** New York, Los Angeles, London, Hong Kong
**Editions** North America, Europe, Asia
**Readers** 4,000,000 worldwide
**Comes out** monthly
**Main subjects** ● fashion ● food ● health ● travel

### Novina

*Novina* is published by Canapub, an international publishing company based in Toronto, Canada. It also has offices in New York, Los Angeles, London and Hong Kong.

There are three editions of the magazine: North America, Europe and Asia. There are 4 million readers worldwide.

*Novina* comes out monthly.

The magazine deals with fashion, food, health and travel.

**B** *Lystra* is a competitor to *Novina*. Read the extract from a trade magazine and write a similar report about *Lystra*.

**LYSTRA**

**Publishers** Cosima Publishing Ltd., London
**Offices** Madrid, Paris, Frankfurt
**Editions** UK, Europe
**Readers** 800,000
**Comes out** weekly
**Main subjects** ● fashion ● food

### Lystra

'Lystra' is published by ...

**Letter**

**A** **Look at the ways to begin and end a letter.**

> **Openings**
>
> If you know the name of the person you're writing to, you can say: *Dear Mr Solano / Dear Ms Ramsden,*
>
> If you don't know their name, you can say: *Dear Sir or Madam,*
>
> **Endings**
>
> *Yours sincerely,* 🇬🇧　　*Sincerely,* 🇺🇸　　*Yours, Yours faithfully,*

**B** **Read the beginning of this letter. Then put the rest of the letter in the correct order.**

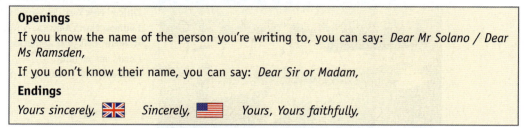

**AMR**

Avenida Asamblea 340
Buenos Aires, Argentina
Tel +54 11 4343 5020, Fax +54 11 4343 5032

Ms Charlotte Ramsden
Canapub Inc.
550 Bloor Street
Toronto, ON, Canada

12 March 200-

Dear Ms Ramsden,

**a** ☐ for *Novina*. As you will see, the results are

**b** ☐ 1 Please find enclosed our market research report

**c** ☐ please do not hesitate to contact me.

**d** ☐ Francisco Solano
Head of Research

Encl: Market Research Report

**e** ☐ very good – there is a very big market for your magazine in Latin America.

**f** ☐ I hope the report answers all your questions. If not,

**g** ☐ Yours sincerely,
*Francisco Solano*

**C** **Match the words to their definitions.**

1 invoice     a an example of a product sent to a customer so they can see it

      b a document with details of an amount of money that someone must pay for products or services

2 report

3 cheque 🇬🇧, check 🇺🇸   c a document about a particular subject

      d a printed piece of paper from a bank that you write on in order to pay someone

4 product sample

**D** **Write a letter to someone outside your organisation, enclosing a document or product sample. In the letter, say what you are enclosing and why you are enclosing it.**

**Report**

**A** Look at the figures from the market research report produced by AMR for *Novina* magazine.

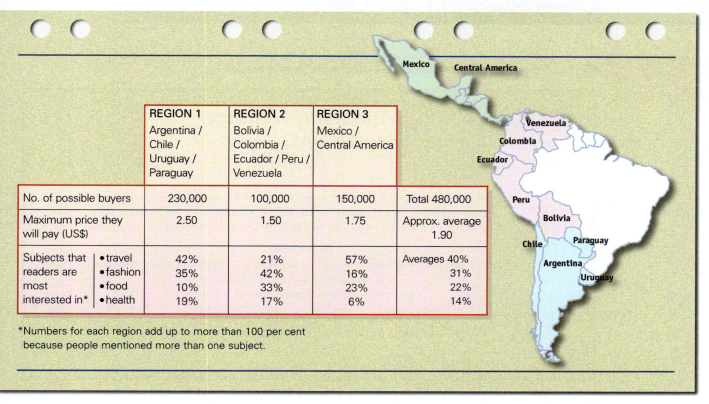

| | | REGION 1<br>Argentina /<br>Chile /<br>Uruguay /<br>Paraguay | REGION 2<br>Bolivia /<br>Colombia /<br>Ecuador / Peru /<br>Venezuela | REGION 3<br>Mexico /<br>Central America | |
|---|---|---|---|---|---|
| No. of possible buyers | | 230,000 | 100,000 | 150,000 | Total 480,000 |
| Maximum price they will pay (US$) | | 2.50 | 1.50 | 1.75 | Approx. average 1.90 |
| Subjects that readers are most interested in* | • travel<br>• fashion<br>• food<br>• health | 42%<br>35%<br>10%<br>19% | 21%<br>42%<br>33%<br>17% | 57%<br>16%<br>23%<br>6% | Averages 40%<br>31%<br>22%<br>14% |

*Numbers for each region add up to more than 100 per cent because people mentioned more than one subject.

**B** Now complete the extract from the report.

We interviewed people in different regions in Latin America. We asked them if they were interested in a magazine like *Novina*. As the table above shows, there is a total possible market of 480,000: the biggest market is Region 1 with [1] 230,000 possible readers. Next is [2]_____ with [3]_____ readers and then comes [4]_____ with [5]_____ . This gives a total of [6]_____ possible readers.

The price they will pay varies from [7]_____ to [8]_____ . I advise you to charge the average of these figures – [9]_____ .

Possible readers are most interested in [10]_____ , especially in Region 3, so I suggest you have lots of articles about this subject. The second most popular subject is [11]_____ . People are least interested in [12]_____ , especially in [13]_____ , so I advise you not to have articles about health in your magazine.

**C** Write a similar report about a possible new market for one of your company's products. (Invent figures if you don't know them.)

Your report should answer these questions:
- What are the main possible sales regions? How much can you sell in each region?
- How much will they pay in each region?
- What is it about the product that is most important in each region?

## Job advertisement

**A** Read the advertisement for a marketing manager at Canapub Inc.

**Canapub Inc**

## Marketing Manager
Salary: 70,000 US$ per year minimum

### *Novina*

is a best-selling magazine for women. We have 4 million readers in Europe, North America and Asia, and now we are launching an edition in Latin America.
We're looking for a marketing manager, based in Buenos Aires, to build this new edition.

**You must:**
- have 10 years' experience in a similar job in marketing in newspapers or magazines.
- speak Spanish and English fluently.
- be free to move to Buenos Aires immediately.

**Please e-mail or fax your résumé to:**
Charlotte Ramsden, chief editor, charlotte.ramsden@canapub.com
Fax +1 416 213 8495

**B** Write a short advertisement for a job in your department (perhaps yours!).

Include details of:
- your company and what it does.
- the job you are advertising.
- the sort of person you are looking for.
- what they must send.
- who they must contact.

CV – 🇬🇧
résumé – 🇺🇸

## Job application

**A** Read Alvaro Mendoza's résumé and e-mail.

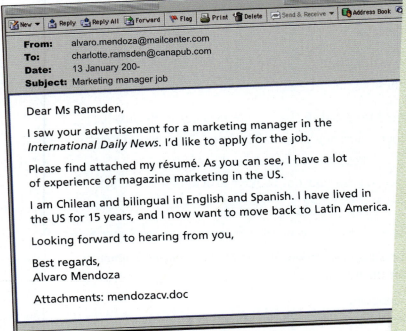

| From: | alvaro.mendoza@mailcenter.com |
|---|---|
| To: | charlotte.ramsden@canapub.com |
| Date: | 13 January 200- |
| Subject: | Marketing manager job |

Dear Ms Ramsden,

I saw your advertisement for a marketing manager in the *International Daily News*. I'd like to apply for the job.

Please find attached my résumé. As you can see, I have a lot of experience of magazine marketing in the US.

I am Chilean and bilingual in English and Spanish. I have lived in the US for 15 years, and I now want to move back to Latin America.

Looking forward to hearing from you,

Best regards,
Alvaro Mendoza

Attachments: mendozacv.doc

### Alvaro Mendoza

**Qualifications**
Degree in English literature, University of Santiago de Chile, *1983–6*
Journalist, *Diario de Santiago*, *1986–90*
MBA, University of Chicago, *1990–91*

**Work experience**
Marketing manager, Scientific Publishing, *1991–now* (in charge of five popular science magazines)

**Nationality** Chilean

**Languages** Spanish, English

**Interests** food, cinema, skiing

**Personal details**
**Date of birth** September 3, 1965
**Address** 130 East 61st St
New York, NY 10021
Tel. 212-329-8734
E-mail: alvaro.mendoza@mailcenter.com

**B** Look at Luisa Barcarem's résumé and complete the e-mail. Put the verbs in brackets in the correct form and add other words as necessary.

---

New ▼ | Reply | Reply All | Forward | Flag | Print | Delete | Send & Receive ▼ | Address Book | Find

**From:** luisa.barcarem@hotmail.com
**To:** charlotte.ramsden@canapub.com
**Date:** 15 January 200-
**Subject:** Marketing manager job

Dear Ms Ramsden,

I ¹_saw_ (see) the job ²_of_ Marketing Manager advertised ³_____ the *International Daily News*. I'd like ⁴_____ _____ (apply) ⁵_____ the job.

Please find attached ⁶_____ résumé. I ⁷_____ (have) a lot ⁸_____ experience ⁹_____ the magazine publishing industry. My qualifications include ¹⁰_____ degree ¹¹_____ Economics from Rio University and an MBA ¹²_____ Miami University. I ¹³_____ (speak) Spanish ¹⁴_____ English fluently.

I ¹⁵_____ (move) ¹⁶_____ the US in 1993 ¹⁷_____ personal reasons, but I now want ¹⁸_____ _____ (return) ¹⁹_____ South America.

Looking ²⁰_____ to hearing ²¹_____ you.

Best regards,

Luisa Barcarem

Attachment: barcarem1.doc

---

## Luisa Barcarem

### Qualifications
- Degree in Economics, University of Rio de Janeiro, 1988–93
- Advertising sales assistant, Latino-America Magazines (LAM), Miami, 1993–96
- Advertising sales manager, LAM, 1996–2000
- MBA, Miami University Business School, 2000–01

### Experience
Marketing manager, Hispano Publishing, 2001–now (in charge of marketing 30 Spanish- and Portuguese-language magazines)

### Nationality
Brazilian

### Languages
Portuguese, Spanish, English

### Interests
opera, swimming, salsa dancing

### PERSONAL DETAILS
**Date of birth**
July 31, 1970

**Address**
6721 South Merrill Ave
Chicago, IL 60649
Tel. 305-742-8532
E-mail:
*luisa.barcarem@hotmail.com*

---

**C** Now write your own CV/résumé.

**D** What's the best order for a CV/résumé? Do you start with what you are doing now and go back? Or do you start with your qualifications and go forward? (Give your reasons.)

**E-mail exchange**

**A** Look at the ways to begin and end an e-mail.

> **Openings**
>
> If you don't know the person very well, you can start as in a letter.
> *Dear Mr ...,* or *Dear Ms ...,*
>
> If you know them better, you can start with their first name.
> *Dear Francisco / Dear Charlotte,*
>
> If you know them even better, you can write *Hello* or *Hi*.
> *Hi, Francisco,*
>
> **Endings**    More formal ➤ Less formal
> *Regards,    Best regards,    All best wishes,    Best wishes,    All the best,    Best,*

**B** Put the extracts from e-mails between Charlotte Ramsden and Luisa Barcarem in order. There are three from Charlotte to Luisa and three from Luisa to Charlotte.

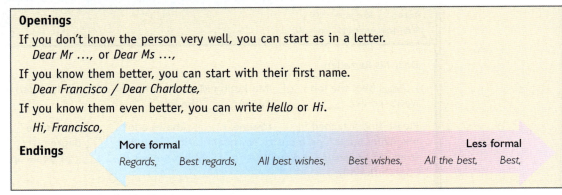

a ☐ Thank you for your e-mail inviting me to an interview. Unfortunately I have a very important meeting on Monday December 2nd. Is another day possible?

b ☐ Please find attached my résumé again. I hope you can open it this time.

c ☐ Thanks for sending your résumé again – I can read it now! Your background is very interesting. Can you come for an interview in Toronto on Monday December 2nd at 2.00 pm?

d ☐ Fine. I can now come to Toronto on Monday December 2nd.

e ☐ I'm traveling all week from Tuesday 3rd December, so Monday is the only possible day for the interview.

f ☐1 Thank you for your e-mail. Unfortunately I couldn't open the attachment. Please could you send it again in Word 6? Many thanks.

**C** Antonia Criado has applied for a job in your department. You invite her for an interview. Write the e-mails in this exchange.

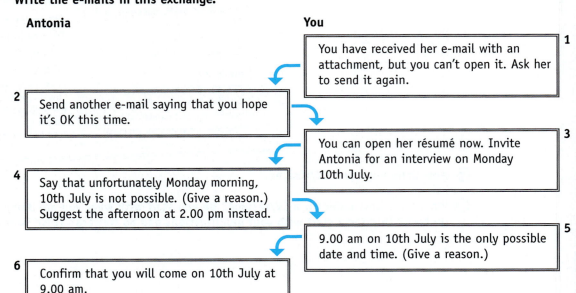

**Antonia** | **You**

1 You have received her e-mail with an attachment, but you can't open it. Ask her to send it again.

2 Send another e-mail saying that you hope it's OK this time.

3 You can open her résumé now. Invite Antonia for an interview on Monday 10th July.

4 Say that unfortunately Monday morning, 10th July is not possible. (Give a reason.) Suggest the afternoon at 2.00 pm instead.

5 9.00 am on 10th July is the only possible date and time. (Give a reason.)

6 Confirm that you will come on 10th July at 9.00 am.

**E-mail**

**(A)** **Read the e-mail.**

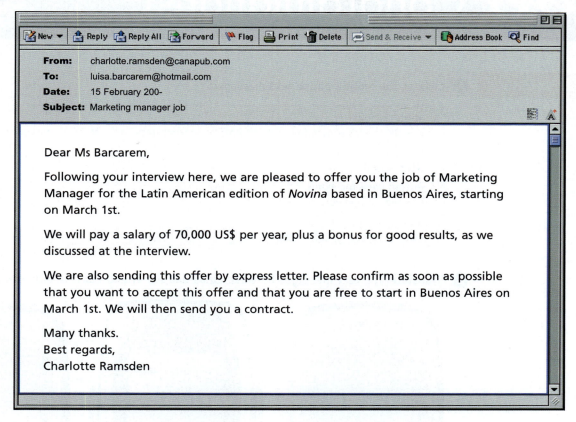

> **New** ▼  |  **Reply**  **Reply All**  **Forward**  |  **Flag**  |  **Print**  **Delete**  |  **Send & Receive** ▼  |  **Address Book**  **Find**
>
> **From:**   charlotte.ramsden@canapub.com
> **To:**   luisa.barcarem@hotmail.com
> **Date:**   15 February 200-
> **Subject:** Marketing manager job
>
> Dear Ms Barcarem,
>
> Following your interview here, we are pleased to offer you the job of Marketing Manager for the Latin American edition of *Novina* based in Buenos Aires, starting on March 1st.
>
> We will pay a salary of 70,000 US$ per year, plus a bonus for good results, as we discussed at the interview.
>
> We are also sending this offer by express letter. Please confirm as soon as possible that you want to accept this offer and that you are free to start in Buenos Aires on March 1st. We will then send you a contract.
>
> Many thanks.
> Best regards,
> Charlotte Ramsden

**(B)** **Luisa writes an e-mail reply to Charlotte. Put the steps in order.**

**a** ☐  Accept the salary.

**b** ☐  End politely.

**c** ☐  Say you can start on March 1st.

**d** ☐ I  Thank Charlotte for offering you the job.

**e** ☐  Say you look forward to receiving the contract.

**(C)** **Now write Luisa's reply.**

**(D)** **Charlotte sends an e-mail back to Luisa. Put the steps in order.**

**a** ☐  End politely.

**b** ☐  Say you look forward to seeing her in Buenos Aires on March 1st.

**c** ☐ I  Thank Luisa for her e-mail.

**d** ☐  Say you will send the contract by FedEx courier.

**e** ☐  You will be in Buenos Aires from March to September to prepare for the September launch of the Latin American edition of *Novina*.

**(E)** **Now write Charlotte's reply.**

**(F)** **Write an e-mail to someone offering them a job in your organisation – giving salary, starting date, etc. Then write an e-mail with that person's reply, saying that they accept the offer.**

# 35 Congratulations!

Text message

**A** Look at the mobile phone text messages.

- abbreviations
  K = OK     EVE = evening     CONGRATS = congratulations     MKTG = marketing
- unusual spellings
  NITE = night
- letters used for words
  C = see     U = you
- numbers used for words
  4GET = forget     L8R = later

**B** 'Translate' the text messages between Luisa and her friend Clarissa into ordinary English.

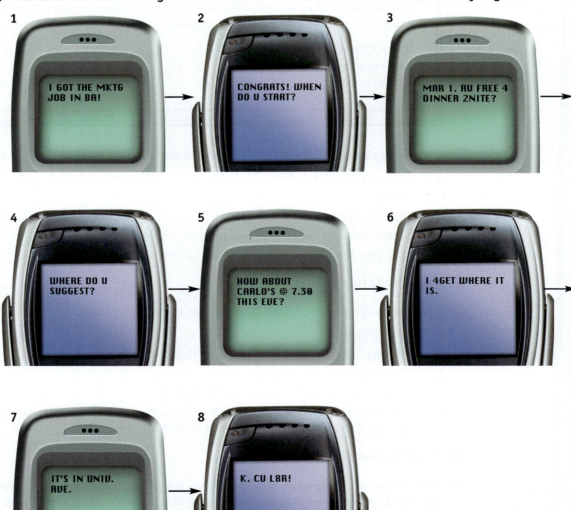

1
I GOT THE MKTG JOB IN BA!

2
CONGRATS! WHEN DO U START?

3
MAR 1. RU FREE 4 DINNER 2NITE?

4
WHERE DO U SUGGEST?

5
HOW ABOUT CARLO'S @ 7.30 THIS EVE?

6
I 4GET WHERE IT IS.

7
IT'S IN UNIV. AVE.

8
K. CU L8R!

**C** Text a friend with some good news and ask them to meet you somewhere this evening. Write the exchange of text messages.

I ...

CONGRATS! ...

**Emoticons**

**A** The day after they have dinner together, Clarissa sends Luisa a text message. Read the message, then match the emoticons to their meanings.

GOOD 2 C U LAST NITE @ CARLO'S :-9 CONGRATS AGAIN ON YR NEW JOB :-) MY BOSS IS VERY ANGRY THIS

MORNING. :-@ THERE ARE PROBLEMS IN THE COMPANY :-X I LIKE IT HERE. I DON'T WANT TO LEAVE MY JOB :-(

TALK 2 U L8R.

| | | |
|---|---|---|
| **1** :-) | **a** | angry |
| **2** :-( | **b** | delicious! |
| **3** :-D | **c** | happy |
| **4** :-C | **d** | I can't say anything |
| **5** :-@ | **e** | I don't know what to say |
| **6** :-9 | **f** | laughing |
| **7** :-X | **g** | sad |
| **8** :-& | **h** | very sad |

**B** Now write a text message to a friend, using four emoticons.

# 36 You're doing a great job!

**Report**

**A** **Look at the graph expressions.**

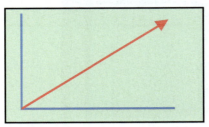

rise / go up

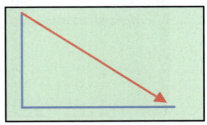

fall / go down

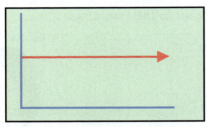

stay the same

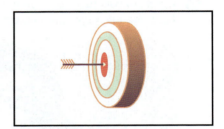

reach a target

**B** **Read the report and complete the graph with the information.**

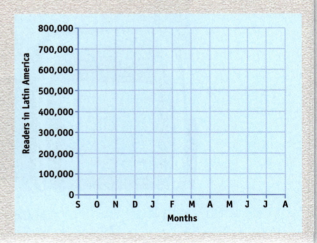

## Canapub Inc    REPORT

**From:** Luisa Barcarem, Buenos Aires office
**To:** Charlotte Ramsden, Toronto office
**Re:** *Novina*
**Date:** August 31 200-

As you can see in the graph, we started in September last year with 100,000 readers. This stayed the same for the next two months. Then in December, the number of readers rose to 250,000. During the following four months, the number of readers rose very quickly to 400,000 in April. Sales stayed the same in May and June. The number of readers started to rise again in July, and in August we reached our target of 600,000.

**C** **Write a report with a graph about numbers of something in your work in the last week, month or year.**

For example, talk about numbers of:
- e-mails sent and received.
- customers.
- products sold.

## E-mail

**A** Read the e-mail.

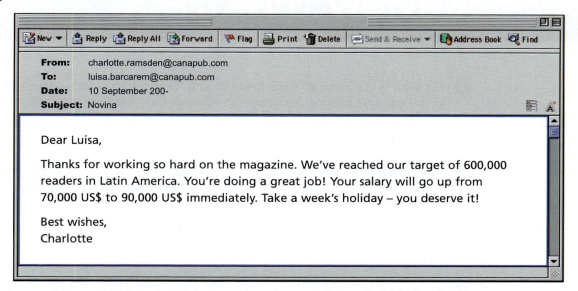

From: charlotte.ramsden@canapub.com
To: luisa.barcarem@canapub.com
Date: 10 September 200-
Subject: Novina

Dear Luisa,

Thanks for working so hard on the magazine. We've reached our target of 600,000 readers in Latin America. You're doing a great job! Your salary will go up from 70,000 US$ to 90,000 US$ immediately. Take a week's holiday – you deserve it!

Best wishes,
Charlotte

**B** Now write one of the following e-mails.

To:

- a colleague. Thank them for helping to finish some work. Offer to take them out to lunch.
- a customer. Thank them for a large order. You will give them a discount on their next order.
- a supplier. Thank them for supplying something (say what it is) on time. You will contact them first the next time that you want something similar.

## Postcard

**A** Read the postcard from Luisa to Clarissa.

ACAPULCO

Hi, Clarissa!
We reached the sales target for the first year for Novina, and I'm here in Acapulco for a break. As you can see in the picture, it's beautiful. The weather is hot, the food is fantastic and the hotel is very comfortable.

Wish you were here!

Love,
Luisa

Clarissa Jensen
349 King Street
Toronto, ON
M5C 1Z9
Canada

**B** You are on holiday. Write a postcard to a friend at work.

# Review 31–36

**A** You work in the accounts department at AMR. Send a letter with an invoice to the head of the accounts payable department at Canapub Inc. (You don't know their name.)

- In your letter, say what you are enclosing – an invoice for $25,000 payable in 30 days.
- End politely.

**B** Two months later, the invoice has still not been paid. You now know that the head of accounts payable at Canapub is Mr Paul Rousseau. Send another copy of the invoice, and say what you are enclosing.

- Ask for payment as soon as possible.
- Say that if he has any questions, he should not hesitate to contact you.
- End politely.

**C** A year after the launch of *Novina* in Latin America, Charlotte Ramsden writes to Francisco Solano of AMR. Put the words in each line into the correct order.

Francisco Dear,

said You were there 600,000 readers possible in America Latin.

We now reached have this target.

report research right was Your.

Thank very you much for work your all it on.

certainly We will with work you the in future new editions on.

best All wishes,

Charlotte

**D** Match the text message abbreviations to their meanings.

| | | | |
|---|---|---|---|
| 1 | 2MORO | a | Lots of love |
| 2 | GR8 | b | before |
| 3 | ME2 | c | work |
| 4 | 2DAY | d | Great! |
| 5 | B4 | e | me too |
| 6 | LOL | f | message |
| 7 | MSG | g | sorry |
| 8 | SRY | h | thanks |
| 9 | THX | i | today |
| 10 | WRK | j | tomorrow |

**E** Clarissa has been in Buenos Aires visiting her friend Luisa Barcarem.
When she leaves, she texts Luisa from the airport.
Translate her text message into ordinary English.

I'M SENDING THIS MSG B4 I GET ON THE PLANE. THX 4 A GR8 TIME IN BA. SRY I COULDN'T STAY LONGER.

IT'LL B DIFFICULT 2 WRK 2MORO! LOL, C.

**F** It's seven years later. Complete the report by the boss of *Novina* in Buenos Aires, using the information in the diagram.

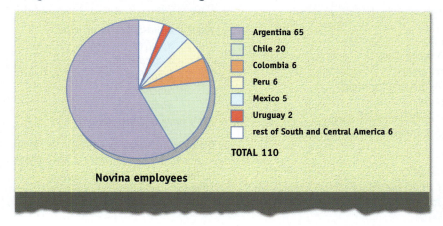

| | |
|---|---|
| Argentina | 65 |
| Chile | 20 |
| Colombia | 6 |
| Peru | 6 |
| Mexico | 5 |
| Uruguay | 2 |
| rest of South and Central America | 6 |

**TOTAL 110**

**Novina employees**

110 people work at the Novina office in Buenos Aires. The biggest group is from Argentina – there are 65 Argentinians. This is normal, as Buenos Aires is in Argentina! Next comes ...

**G** Write a report about the number of employees at *Novina* in Buenos Aires over the last seven years, using the information in the diagram.

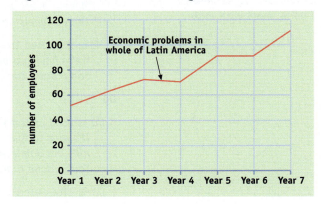

Economic problems in whole of Latin America

In Year 1, we started with 51 employees. The number rose to 62 in Year 2 ...

# Vocabulary builder

When you work on vocabulary, don't just think about individual words. Think about how words go together – how a word typically goes with certain other words. When you write down vocabulary, note down some of these typical combinations.

For example, don't just write down the word *market*, note down:

- expressions: *a new market, a difficult market*
- complete sentences: *Supersport has moved into the US market.*

---

## Word combinations: *have*

- Look at these 'ordinary' uses of *have* in *Best Practice Elementary*.
    *I have a lot of work to do.*
    *She has a new job at Mimosa Cars.*
    *Do you have a lot of customers?*
    *Most new buildings have air-conditioning.*
    *Do you have a reservation?*
    *I have an appointment with Sven Karlsson.*
    *If you have any questions, please do not hesitate to contact me.*

- *Have* is used to ask for things.
    *Can we have a discount of 15 per cent?*
    *Could we have a table for four?*
    *Can I have a receipt, please?*

- *Have* is often used with food and drink.

| have | a glass/bottle of wine |
|------|------------------------|
|      | a coffee               |
|      | a sandwich             |
|      | breakfast              |
|      | lunch                  |
|      | dinner                 |

    *Let's have a drink tonight.*

- Other expressions with *have* in this book.
    *It's important to have a long break.*
    *Did you have a good journey?*
    *Have a nice stay!*

---

## Word combinations: *make* and *do*

### Make

- *Make* is used to talk about actions with some nouns. These nouns all occur in this book, most with *make*.

| make a/an | arrangement |
|-----------|-------------|
|           | mistake     |
|           | profit/loss |
|           | change      |
|           | note        |
|           | reservation |
|           | decision    |
|           | phone call  |
|           | suggestion  |
|           | enquiry     |
|           | plan        |

- These expressions are often used instead of verbs.
    *Astrid made arrangements to visit Sacramento.*
    = She arranged to visit Sacramento.

    *She made a reservation on a flight to Sacramento.*
    = She reserved a seat on a flight to Sacramento.

- *Make* is also used to talk about producing things.
    *Supersport sells sports goods, but they don't make them.*
    *Make a question with 'do'.*
    *The designers have made new drawings.*

- *Make it* is used to talk about arrangements.
    *We're having a party on Saturday. Hope you can make it!*
    *Sorry, but I can't make it on Tuesday for our meeting.*

### Do

- *Do* is used as a main verb to talk about activities.
    *It's nice to talk, but I must do some work.*
    *ARM are doing research in Latin America.*
    *You've done a great job!*

- *Do* is often used with *-ing* nouns.
    *He does the shopping and I do the cleaning.*

---

## Word combinations: *home*

- Look at these expressions with *home*.
    *I go home at ...*
    *I get home at ...*
    *The postman came, but I wasn't at home.*

    *On weekday evenings, I stay at home – I don't go out.*
    *work from home*

- Note that you don't talk about ~~being at the home~~ or ~~going to the home~~.

## Word combinations: *work* and *job*

- If you *work*, you have a job. But you don't say that someone has ~~a work~~. *Work* is also the place where you do your job.

  I | go to work by bus, by train …
  | leave for work at …
  | get to work at …
  | 'm at work from … to … .
  | 'm off work because I'm ill.

- Note that you don't say ~~to the work~~ or ~~at the work~~.

- Ask and answer questions about jobs like this.

  What's your job (= What do you do?)
  – I'm a/an | accountant.
  | factory worker.
  | researcher.
  | designer.
  | manager.
  | salesman/saleswoman/salesperson/sales rep.
  | engineer.
  | office worker.
  | personal assistant.

Who do you work for?
– I work for Canapub.
Where do you work?
– I work | in a factory/shop/office/showroom.
| at the head office.
Which department do you work in?
– I work in the | sales | department.
| accounts |
| human resources |
| production |
| planning |
| marketing |
What does your company/organisation do?
– We make cars. (= We manufacture cars.)
– We produce magazines for the Latin American market.
– It distributes saunas.
– It sells sporting goods.

## Core business vocabulary

- These important business words occur in *Best Practice Elementary*. Do you know them all? Can you use them?

accounts   advertising   charge (v)   client   competitor   cost (n + v)   customer   delivery   discount   distribution distributor   employee   factory   goods   human resources   invest   investment   invoice   loss   manage   manager manufacture   manufacturer   market (n)   marketing   office   order   pay (n + v)   payment   price   product production   profit (v)   profitable   range   sales   services   ship (n + v)   stock (n)   supplier   supply (v)   warehouse (n)

Bellway **manufactures** computers in its factory outside Dublin.

> Ireland is a great place for **production**. We've **invested** in the most modern computer factory in the world.
>
> **Customers order** by phone or by Internet. So we don't have **stocks** of finished computers sitting in **warehouses** waiting for buyers.
>
> 48 hours after receiving an order, we send the **goods** to the customer. We don't use **distributors** – we **ship** our **products** directly to customers. **Delivery** in most of Europe is the day after the computer leaves the factory.

> Bellway is a very good company to work for. Our **employees** like living in Ireland. Our factory and **offices** are in beautiful country outside Dublin. It's a great place to live!

human resources director

marketing manager

accounts manager

production manager

> And the system is great for the **accounts**. We can check **sales** as they happen. Most individual customers pay by credit card, and the credit card company pays us immediately, so we don't have to wait for **payment** after sending the **invoice**. (Companies can wait 30 days before they pay, but not longer!)
>
> And the **costs** of doing business here are very low. Bellway is the most **profitable** computer company in the world. We've never made a **loss**!

> This **distribution** system is also great for **marketing**. It means that the **prices** that we **charge** are lower than those of our **competitors**. And we offer big **discounts** at times of year when business is usually slow.
>
> We can change our **product range** very fast, and tell our customers about it through **advertising**.
>
> We don't only sell goods – we also sell **services**. For example, if the customer pays more, the delivery driver can prepare the customer's computer and check that it works OK.

101

## Word combinations: *market*

- These expressions come in front of *market* in *Best Practice Elementary*.

| a | big | market |
|---|-----|--------|
|   | easy |       |
|   | difficult |  |
|   | new |        |
|   | possible |   |
|   | total |      |
| the | United States | |
|   | US sporting goods | |

- Now look at these combinations.
  a total possible market of 580,000
  the biggest market in the world

- *enter*, *leave* and *move into* are some of the verbs used in front of *market*.
  Supersport has moved into the US market.
  Canapub has entered the Latin American market.

## Word combinations: nouns and verbs

- Look at these examples of verbs that can typically come in front of some of the nouns from the core business vocabulary on page 101.

phone a customer       order new stock
make a delivery        pay an invoice
open a factory         charge x dollars

- Now look at nouns that typically follow some of the verbs from the core business vocabulary.

cost x euros           manage a department
invest in new equipment  pay a supplier
supply goods           ship products

## Telephone/e-mail language

### Asking for someone
*Can I speak to Mr Bashir, please?*
*Is Alessandra Tivoli there?*
*Can I speak to someone in sales, please?*

### Saying who you are
*This is Mick (speaking).*
*Paolo Ponte here.*
*I'm calling/phoning from Mimosa Cars in Italy.*

### Asking for the caller's name
*Who's calling, please?*
*How do you spell your name, please?*
*Can you say that again, please?*

### Asking the caller to wait
*Hold on, please.*
*Hold the line, please.*
*Please hold.*
*Would you like to hold?*
*– OK. I'll hold. / No thanks. I'll call back later.*

### Offering help
*Sorry to keep you waiting.*
*Can I help?*
*How can I help?*

### If the person is not available
*Sorry – the line's busy.*
*I'm sorry, but he isn't here today.*
*Sven Karlsson is in a meeting / out of the office / on holiday.*
*Can I take a message? / Would you like to leave a message?*

### Leaving a message
*Can you give him a message?*
*I'm phoning/calling about ...*
*Can he call/phone me tomorrow, please?*
*Can you ask him to call/phone me back?*
*Can he send me an e-mail?*
*I have a problem for Wednesday afternoon. Can he call/phone me back so we can fix another time?*

### Confirming details
*I'll give him/her the message. So, (just) to check the details. Your surname is Baxter: B-A-X-T-E-R.*
*– That's right. / That's it.*

### Telephone alphabet
If you want to spell a word, you can say, for example, 'C for Charlie' or 'C as in Charlie'. This list shows words often used for this, but you can use your own names or words.

| | | | |
|---|---|---|---|
| **A**pple | **H**otel | **O**scar | **U**niform |
| **B**ravo | **I**ndia | **P**apa | **V**ictor |
| **C**harlie | **J**uliet | **Q**uebec | **W**hisky |
| **D**elta | **K**ilo | **R**omeo | **X**-ray |
| **E**cho | **L**ima | **S**ierra | **Y**ankee |
| **F**oxtrot | **M**ike | **T**ango | **Z**ulu |
| **G**olf | **N**ovember | | |

### Phone numbers
Write: 00  1  212  734  892  3020
Say:  oh-oh  one  two-one-two  seven-three-four eight-nine-two  three-oh-two-oh 🇬🇧
or:  zero-zero  one  two-one-two  seven-three-four eight-nine-two  three-zero-two-zero 🇺🇸

Write: 744 2899
Say:  seven-double-four  two-eight-double-nine 🇬🇧
or:  seven-four-four  two-eight-nine-nine 🇺🇸

### E-mail addresses
Write: paolo.ponte@mimosa.it
Say:  Paolo dot Ponte at Mimosa dot I T

Write: Sven dot Karlsson at splashpools dot co dot uk
or:
Write: Sven dot Karlsson – Karlsson with a K and two Ss – at splashpools – splashpools all one word – dot co dot uk

## Numbers

| | | | |
|---|---|---|---|
| 1 one | 1st* first | | |
| 2 two | 2nd* second | | |
| 3 three | 3rd* third | | |
| 4 four | 4th fourth | | |
| 5 five | 5th fifth | | |
| 6 six | 6th sixth | | |
| 7 seven | 7th seventh | | |
| 8 eight | 8th eighth | | |
| 9 nine | 9th ninth | | |
| 10 ten | 10th tenth | | |
| 11 eleven | 11th eleventh | | |
| 12 twelve | 12th twelfth | | |
| 13 thirteen | 13th thirteenth | | |
| 14 fourteen | 14th fourteenth | | |
| 15 fifteen | 15th fifteenth | | |
| 16 sixteen | 16th sixteenth | | |
| 17 seventeen | 17th seventeenth | | |
| 18 eighteen | 18th eighteenth | | |
| 19 nineteen | 19th nineteenth | | |
| 20 twenty | 20th twentieth | | |
| 21 twenty-one | 21st* twenty-first | | |
| 22 twenty-two | 22nd* twenty-second | | |
| 23 twenty-three | 23rd* twenty-third | | |
| 30 thirty | 30th thirtieth | | |
| 31 thirty-one | 31st* thirty-first | | |
| 40 forty | 40th fortieth | | |
| 50 fifty | 50th fiftieth | | |
| 60 sixty | 60th sixtieth | | |
| 70 seventy | 70th seventieth | | |
| 80 eighty | 80th eightieth | | |
| 90 ninety | 90th ninetieth | | |
| 100 a hundred | 100th hundredth | | |

120  a hundred and twenty, one hundred and twenty
one hundred twenty

200 two hundred (not ~~two hundreds~~)

1,000 a thousand, one thousand

2,000 two thousand (not ~~two thousands~~)

- When you give a specific figure, you say *two hundred euros* (not ~~two hundred of euros~~).

- But when there is no specific figure, you use *of*.
  *hundreds of euros*
  *thousands of people*
  *millions of dollars*

- When you don't give an exact figure, you can use *about*.
  *About 3 million people live in Latvia.*

### Dates

- *Be careful with these abbreviations when you write dates. Don't write ~~1th, 2th, 3th, 21th~~ etc!

- Say: *the 31st of March* or *March the 31st* 🇬🇧,
  *March thirty-first* 🇺🇸

- Write: *31st March, 31 March, March 31st,* or *March 31* (only the last two are used in the US)

### Streets

- In the US, streets are often described like this.
  *Where's the New York State Theater?*
  *– On West 62nd Street between 9th Avenue and 10th Avenue.*

### Floors

- In the US, when you go through the front door of a building, you are normally on the *first floor*; in Britain, you are on the *ground floor*.
  *There are great views from the top floor of the Swiss Re building in London (not the ~~last floor~~).*

## Countries, adjectives, capitals

### European Union

| Country | Adjective | Capital |
|---|---|---|
| Austria | Austrian | Vienna |
| Belgium | Belgian | Brussels |
| Cyprus | Cypriot | Nicosia |
| Czech Republic | Czech | Prague |
| Denmark | Danish | Copenhagen |
| Estonia | Estonian | Tallinn |
| Finland | Finnish | Helsinki |
| France | French | Paris |
| Germany | German | Berlin |
| Greece | Greek | Athens |
| Hungary | Hungarian | Budapest |
| Ireland | Irish | Dublin |
| Italy | Italian | Rome |
| Latvia | Latvian | Riga |
| Lithuania | Lithuanian | Vilnius |
| Luxembourg | — | Luxembourg |
| Malta | Maltese | Valetta |
| Netherlands | Dutch | The Hague |
| Portugal | Portuguese | Lisbon |
| Slovakia | Slovakian | Bratislava |
| Slovenia | Slovenian | Ljubljana |
| Spain | Spanish | Madrid |
| Sweden | Swedish | Stockholm |
| Poland | Polish | Warsaw |
| United Kingdom* | — | London |

### *Countries of the UK

| | | |
|---|---|---|
| England | English | London |
| Wales | Welsh | Cardiff |
| Scotland | Scottish | Edinburgh |
| Northern Ireland | Northern Irish | Belfast |

England + Wales + Scotland = Great Britain.
The adjective = British.

### Some other European countries

| | | |
|---|---|---|
| Switzerland | Swiss | Berne |
| Norway | Norwegian | Oslo |
| Russia** | Russian | Moscow |

**Of course, a lot of Russia is in Asia!

### Some Asian countries

| Country | Adjective | Capital |
|---|---|---|
| China | Chinese | Beijing |
| India | Indian | New Delhi |
| Japan | Japanese | Tokyo |
| Malaysia | Malaysian | Kuala Lumpur |
| Pakistan | Pakistani | Islamabad |
| Taiwan | Taiwanese | Taipei |
| Indonesia | Indonesian | Jakarta |
| Philippines | Philippine | Manila |
| Singapore | Singaporean | Singapore |
| South Korea | South Korean | Seoul |

### Australasia

| | | |
|---|---|---|
| Australia | Australian | Canberra |
| New Zealand | — | Auckland |

### Some North African countries

| | | |
|---|---|---|
| Morocco | Moroccan | Rabat |
| Tunisia | Tunisian | Tunis |
| Egypt | Egyptian | Cairo |

### Some other African countries

| | | |
|---|---|---|
| Kenya | Kenyan | Nairobi |
| Nigeria | Nigerian | Abuja |
| South Africa | South African | Pretoria |

### North America

| | | |
|---|---|---|
| Canada | Canadian | Quebec |
| United States | American | Washington, DC |

### Some countries in Latin America

| | | |
|---|---|---|
| Argentina | Argentinean | Buenos Aires |
| Brazil | Brazilian | Brasilia |
| Chile | Chilean | Santiago |
| Mexico | Mexican | Mexico City |

# Grammar overview

## Verbs

### Present simple

*be*

| Affirmative | Negative | Questions |
|---|---|---|
| I'm (am) … | I'm not (am not) … | Am I? |
| You're (are) … | You aren't (are not) … | Are you? |
| He \| | He \| | \| he? |
| She \| 's (is) … | She \| isn't (is not) … | Is \| she? |
| It \| | It \| | \| it? |
| We're (are) … | We aren't (are not) … | Are we? |
| They're (are) … | They aren't (are not) … | Are they? |

**Other regular verbs**

| Affirmative | Negative | Questions |
|---|---|---|
| I work. | I don't (do not) work. | Do I work? |
| You work. | You don't (do not) work. | Do you work? |
| He \| | He \| | \| he |
| She \| works. | She \| doesn't (does not) work. | Does \| she \| work? |
| It \| | It \| | \| it |
| We work. | We don't (do not) work. | Do we work? |
| They work. | They don't (do not) work. | Do they work? |

### Form

- For *be* and regular verbs, see above.
- With *go* and *do*, and with verbs ending in *-ch*, *-ss*, *-sh* and *-x*, add *-es* to the base form of the verb.
    *The truck goes to Gothenburg.*
    *The ferry crosses the North Sea.*

### *Wh-* questions

- With *I, you, we, they*, you make *Wh-* questions with *do*.
    *Where do you make the saunas?*
- With *he/she/it*, you make *Wh-* questions with *does*.
    *When does the ferry leave?*

### Use

You use the present simple:

- to talk about general facts.
    *Marc teaches in a school in Pau.*
- to talk about customs, habits and routines.
    *Douglas usually has lunch at 12.45.*
- to talk about personal characteristics.
    *Fiona likes the country because it's so quiet.*
- to describe processes.
    *The truck drives onto the ferry. It drives off the next morning.*

## Present continuous

| Affirmative | Negative | Questions |
|---|---|---|
| I'm (am) working. | I'm not (am not) working. | Am I working? |
| You're (are) working. | You aren't (are not) working. | Are you working? |
| He | He | he |
| She 's (is) working. | She isn't (is not) working. | Is she working? |
| It | It | it |
| We're (are) working. | We aren't (are not) working. | Are we working? |
| They're (are) working. | They aren't (are not) working. | Are they working? |

### Form

- You make the present continuous with *be* + the *-ing* form of the verb.
- *-ing* endings:
  — most regular verbs: add *-ing* to the base form of the verb
    *do – doing*
    *think – thinking*
  — verbs ending in *-e*: drop the *-e* and add *-ing*
    *drive – driving*
    *hope – hoping*
    *taste – tasting*
  — verbs ending in a vowel and a consonant: double the consonant and add *-ing*
    *hit – hitting*
    *win – winning*
  — verbs ending in a vowel or *-y* or *-w*: add *-ing*
    *ski – skiing*
    *play – playing*

### Question words

*How are you paying?   What is he doing?   Where is she going?*

### Use

You use the present continuous:

- to talk about what is happening now.
  *He's driving onto the ferry.*
- to talk about temporary situations.
  *It's difficult to park because they're working on the road.*
  (You can say this in the evening too, when the work has stopped for the day.)
- to talk about future plans that are quite certain, for example travel plans.
  *We're leaving for France tomorrow.*

## Past simple

*be*

| Affirmative | Negative | Questions |
|---|---|---|
| I was ... | I wasn't (was not) ... | Was I? |
| You were ... | You weren't (were not) ... | Were you? |
| He | He | he? |
| She was ... | She wasn't (was not) ... | Was she? |
| It | It | it? |
| We were ... | We weren't (were not) ... | Were we? |
| They were ... | They weren't (were not) ... | Were they? |

**Regular verbs**

| Affirmative | | Negative | | Questions | | |
|---|---|---|---|---|---|---|
| I<br>You<br>He<br>She<br>It<br>We<br>They | worked. | I<br>You<br>He<br>She<br>It<br>We<br>They | didn't (did not) work. | Did | I<br>you<br>he<br>she<br>it<br>we<br>they | work? |

**Form**

- Most regular verbs: add *-ed* to the base form of the verb.
  *talk – talked*
  *work – worked*
- Verbs ending in *-e*: add *-d*.
  *hope – hoped*
  *decide – decided.*
- Verbs of one syllable ending in a vowel and a consonant: double the consonant and add *-ed*.
  *plan – planned*
  *stop – stopped*
- Verbs ending in *-y*: drop the *-y* and add *-ied*.
  *carry – carried   study – studied*
- Verbs ending in a vowel + *-y*: add *-ed*.
  *delay – delayed*
  *play – played*
- For irregular verbs, see page 110.

**Question words**

  *Why did you work?   Where did she go?   How did they travel?*

**Pronunciation**

/t/   *talked, stopped, worked*
/d/   *agreed, listened, moved*
/ɪd/ (past simple endings *-ded* and *-ted*)
   *decided   needed   invested   wanted*

**Use**

You use the past simple:

- to talk about events in the past.
  *Fiona moved to France because she wanted a change.*
- when you give a specific time. For example, you always use it with:
  *at (3 o'clock)   yesterday   last week   last month*
  *Where did you go yesterday? – I went to Toulouse.*
  *The race started at 3 o'clock.*

## Present perfect

| Affirmative | | | Negative | | | Questions | | |
|---|---|---|---|---|---|---|---|---|
| I<br>You | have | | I<br>You | haven't (have not) | | Have | I<br>you | |
| He<br>She<br>It | has | worked. | He<br>She<br>It | hasn't (has not) | worked. | Has | he<br>she<br>it | worked? |
| We<br>They | have | | We<br>They | haven't | | Have | you<br>they | |

**Form**

- You make the present perfect with *have* or *has* + the past participle.
- Regular past participles:
  - — most regular verbs ending in *-e*: add *-d*
    *decide – decided*
    *state – stated*
  - — most regular verbs ending in a consonant followed by *-y*: drop the *y* and add *-ied*
    *deny – denied*
    *empty – emptied*
  - — most other regular verbs: add *-ed*
    *talk – talked*
    *play – played*
- For irregular past participles, see page 110.

**Use**

You use the present perfect:

- to talk about recent events.
  *Supersport has opened stores in the US.*
- to talk about past events, for example with *ever* and *never*.
  *Have you ever been to Malaysia? – No, I've never been there.*
- to refer to specific times in the past.
  *I went there last year.*

## Future with *will*

| Affirmative | | | Negative | | | Questions | | |
|---|---|---|---|---|---|---|---|---|
| I<br>You<br>He<br>She<br>It<br>We<br>They | 'll (will) | work. | I<br>You<br>He<br>She<br>It<br>We<br>They | won't (will not) | work. | Will | I<br>you<br>he<br>she<br>it<br>you<br>they | work? |

**Form**

- You make the future simple with *will* and the base form of the verb.

**Question words**

- You make questions with question words like this.
  *When will you leave? How will you travel?*

**Use**

You use *will*:
- to talk about future events.
  *Our sales will increase by 200 per cent.*
- to talk about a decision you make at the time of speaking.
  *I'll phone you this afternoon.*

## Future with *going to*

- You use *going to* and the base form of the verb to talk about future plans and intentions.
  *KL Industries are going to invest in Italy.*
  *Is Paolo going to visit Malaysia?*
  *We aren't going to close the factory in Modena.*

## Modal verbs

- Here are some modal verbs.
  *can   could   must   would*

**Form**

- Modal verbs:
  — don't change their form for different persons.
  *Can she speak Italian?*
  *Could you help me with these figures?*
  — are not used with *do* in questions and negatives.
  *Could we have another bottle of wine?*
  *Customers won't like this product.*
  — are followed by the base form of the verb without *to*.
  *You must finish that by this evening.*
  *Would you take my bags upstairs?*

*can* – **use**

- You use *can*:
  — to talk about possibilities.
  *Our salesman can come on Wednesday morning.*
  — to make offers.
  *Can I help you?*
  — to ask for things.
  *Can you send a brochure?*
- You use *can't* to talk about things you are:
  — not able to do.
  *We can't deliver before next year.*
  — not allowed to do.
  *You can't smoke in here.*

*could* – **use**

- You use *could*:
  — to ask for something politely.
  *Could I have the bill please?*
  — to ask people to do things.
  *Could you get me a coffee, please?*

*must* – **use**

- You use *must* to tell someone in a direct way what to do.
  *In this test, you must answer all the questions.*

- You use *mustn't* to tell someone in a direct way what not to do.
  *You must not talk during the test.*

- You use *don't have to* to say that something is not necessary.
  *You don't have to give your name, but you can if you want to.*

## Verb patterns

Some verbs follow particular patterns. For example:

- to ask someone (not) to do something.
  *She asked him not to smoke in the building.*

- to tell someone (not) to do something.
  *I told them to go home.*

- to advise someone (not) to do something.
  *His doctor advised him to take a holiday.*

- to want someone to do something.
  *I want you to do this today.*

- to agree with someone (about something).
  *He agreed with her about the plan.*

- to disagree with someone (about something).
  *He disagreed with her about the film.*

## Verbs with prepositions

- Some verbs are used with prepositions.
  *I turned on the radio and listened to the news.*
- Sometimes the meaning of a verb changes when it is used with a preposition. Compare these sentences.
  *Please can you check the spelling in this letter for me?*
  *You must check in at least an hour before your flight.*
- Here are some verb + preposition combinations with an object.
  *She picked up the phone and then put it down.*
  *I turned on the heating and then turned it off.*
  *He put his computer in its bag and took it out when he got to the meeting.*

### Word order

- Notice how you can change the word order.
  *She picked the phone up. She picked up the phone.*
- But you must put object pronouns (for example *it*) between the verb and the preposition.
  *She picked it up.*

## Irregular verbs

| Base form | Past tense | Past participle |
|---|---|---|
| be | was/were | been |
| become | became | become |
| begin | began | begun |
| break | broke | broken |
| bring | brought | brought |
| build | built | built |
| buy | bought | bought |
| catch | caught | caught |
| choose | chose | chosen |
| come | came | come |
| cost | cost | cost |
| cut | cut | cut |
| deal | dealt | dealt |
| do | did | done |
| draw | drew | drawn |
| drink | drank | drunk |
| drive | drove | driven |
| eat | ate | eaten |
| fall | fell | fallen |
| feel | felt | felt |
| find | found | found |
| fly | flew | flown |
| forbid | forbade | forbidden |
| forget | forgot | forgotten |
| get | got | got |
| give | gave | given |
| go | went | gone |
| grow | grew | grown |
| have | had | had |
| hear | heard | heard |
| hide | hid | hidden |
| hit | hit | hit |
| hold | held | held |
| hurt | hurt | hurt |
| keep | kept | kept |
| know | knew | known |
| lay | laid | laid |
| lead | led | led |
| learn | learnt/learned | learnt/learned |
| leave | left | left |
| lend | lent | lent |
| let | let | let |

| Base form | Past tense | Past participle |
|---|---|---|
| lie | lay | lain |
| lost | lost | lost |
| make | made | made |
| mean | meant | meant |
| meet | met | met |
| pay | paid | paid |
| quit | quit | quit |
| read | read | read |
| ride | rode | ridden |
| ring | rang | rung |
| rise | rose | risen |
| run | ran | run |
| say | said | said |
| see | saw | seen |
| sell | sold | sold |
| send | sent | sent |
| set | set | set |
| shake | shook | shaken |
| shoot | shot | shot |
| show | showed | shown |
| shut | shut | shut |
| sing | sang | sung |
| sit | sat | sat |
| sleep | slept | slept |
| speak | spoke | spoken |
| spend | spent | spent |
| spread | spread | spread |
| stand | stood | stood |
| steal | stole | stolen |
| stick | stuck | stuck |
| swim | swam | swum |
| take | took | taken |
| teach | taught | taught |
| tell | told | told |
| think | thought | thought |
| throw | threw | thrown |
| understand | understood | understood |
| wear | wore | worn |
| win | won | won |
| write | wrote | written |

# Nouns

## Plurals

### Regular

- Most nouns: add -s.
    *car – cars*
    *product – products*
- Nouns ending in -y: drop the -y and add -ies.
    *company – companies*
    *secretary – secretaries*
- Nouns ending in -o, -ch, -ss, -sh, -x: add -es.
    *sandwich – sandwiches*
    *wish – wishes*

### Irregular

   *man – men*
   *child – children*
   *person – people*
   *woman – women*

### Countable and uncountable nouns

- Some nouns are countable. They have plural forms, as shown above.
    *1 showroom – 2 showrooms, 1 employee – 2 employees*
    *1 person – 2 people, 1 child – 2 children*
- Other nouns are uncountable. They do not have a plural.
    *work   money   free time*

## Other structures with nouns

### a/an

- You use *a*:
  — in front of nouns that begin with a consonant.
    *a house*
  — in front of adjectives before nouns where the adjective begins with a consonant.
    *a powerful car*
- You use *an*:
  — in front of nouns that begin with a vowel.
    *an e-mail*
  — in front of adjectives before nouns where the adjective begins with a vowel.
    *an excellent place to live*
- You use *a/an* when you talk about something for the first time.
    *They have a showroom in Bristol.*
    *He has an office in Modena.*
- You use *a/an* with jobs.
    *He's a postman.*
    *She's an engineer.*

### the

- You use *the*:
  — to talk about something again.
    *The meeting is at 2 o'clock.*
  — when there is only one.
    *the sporting goods market in California*

### there is / there are

- With singular and uncountable nouns, you use *there is* or *there's* in spoken English.
  *Is there an office in Manchester? – No, there isn't. But there's an office in London.*
  *There is a problem with the electricity.*
  *There is a very big market for the magazine in Latin America.*
  *There's a new fish restaurant in town.*
  *There's easy parking in front of the building.*

- With plural nouns you use *there are*.
  *Are there showrooms in Scotland? – No, there aren't. But there are three showrooms in England.*
  *There are 900,000 lawyers in the US, but only 20,000 in Japan.*
  *On a typical day in Europe, there are 17 million meetings.*
  *There are 65 Argentineans at the Novina office.*

- For *there is / there are + some* or *any*, see below.

### much/many/a lot

- With countable nouns, you ask questions with *How many*.
  *How many showrooms are there?*
  *How many visitors do you get?*
  *How many products do you sell?*

- You can answer with:
  — a number: *3 in the UK.   20 a week.   About 200.*
  — or with: *Not many.   Not a lot.   A lot.*

- With countable nouns, you ask questions with *How much*.
  *How much work do you have at the moment?*
  *How much free time do you get?*
  *How much money do you have on you?*

- You can answer with:
  — a quantity: *10 hours a week.   £25.*
  — or with: *Not much.   Not a lot.    A lot.*

- You can also use *a lot* as an adverb.
  *I like it a lot.*

### some and any

- You usually use *some* with uncountable nouns and with plural countable nouns to talk about a quantity of something without being exact.

- You use *some* in affirmative sentences, but not in negative sentences.
  *I can give you some information about these jackets.*
  *We have some maps of Ecuador.*

- You can use *some* in questions – for example, when you ask for something or offer something.
  *Do you have some Japanese bikes?*
  *Would you like some coffee?*

- You use *any* in questions and negative sentences.
  *Do you have any Austrian walking boots?*
  *We don't have any Austrian boots, but we have some Italian boots.*

# Adjectives

## Possessive adjectives

I → *my*   you → *your*   he → *his*   she → *her*   it → *its*   we → *our*   they → *their*
*My name's Alessandra.*

## Comparatives and superlatives

- Adjectives with one syllable: add *-er* for the comparative and *-est* for the superlative.
  *cheap – cheaper – cheapest*
  *fast – faster – faster*

- Adjectives ending in -e: add -r for the comparative and -st for the superlative.
  *large – larger – largest*
  *fine – finer –finest*
- Adjectives ending in -y: add -ier for the comparative and -iest for the superlative.
  *easy – easier – easiest*
  *friendly – friendlier – friendliest*
- One-syllable adjectives: double the consonant and add -er or -est
  *hot – hotter – hottest*
  *sad – sadder – saddest*
- Two syllables or more, not ending in -y: use *more* for the comparative form and *most* for the superlative form of adjectives
  *successful – more successful – most successful*
  *expensive – more expensive – most expensive*
- Some comparative and superlative forms are irregular.
  *good – better – best*
  *bad – worse – worst*
- You use *than* (not *that*) to make comparisons.
  *The X300 is better than the X200.*
- Some adjectives do not have comparative and superlative forms.
  *excellent   wonderful*

# Adverbs

- You usually make an adverb by adding -ly to the adjective.
  *bad – badly*
  *usual – usually*
- With adjectives ending in -y: drop the -y and add -ily.
  *easy – easily*
  *funny – funnily*
- Some adverbs are the same as the adjective.
  *early   late   fast   hard*
- Some adverbs are irregular.
  *good – well*
  *He's a very good driver. He drives very well.*

## Comparatives and superlatives: form

- The comparatives and superlatives of adverbs are usually formed with *more* and *most*.
  *easily – more easily – most easily*
  *efficiently – more efficiently – most efficiently*
- Adverbs that have the same form as adjectives have the same comparatives and superlatives as the adjectives. See above.
- Some adverbs have comparatives and superlatives with *more* and *most* and also with -er and -est.
  *quickly – more quickly – most quickly*
  *quick – quicker – quickest*
- Some comparative and superlative forms are irregular.
  *well – better – best*
  *badly – worse – worst*

### Word order

- Adverbs of frequency *always, often, sometimes, usually, never* go before the verb.
  *I often travel on business.*
  *She never goes on holiday in August.*
- But you put them after *be*.
  *He's always late.*

# Audio script

## Module 1  Introductions

### Unit 1  Where are you from?

**1.1**  **1** *Fiona:* Hi, my name's Fiona Macpherson. I'm from Scotland.

**2** *Alessandra:* Hello, I'm Alessandra Tivoli. I'm from Italy.

**3** *Carole:* I'm Carole Bruckner. I'm from America.

**4** *Saleem:* Hello, my name's Saleem Bashir. I'm from Malaysia – Kuala Lumpur.

**5** *Astrid:* Hi, my name's Astrid Schmidt. I'm from Frankfurt, in Germany.

**6** *Sven:* Hello, I'm Sven Karlsson. I'm from Sweden, from Uppsala.

**1.2**  **1** *Alessandra:* I'm Alessandra Tivoli. I'm from Modena, in Italy.

**2** *Sven:* I'm Sven Karlsson. I'm from Uppsala, in Sweden.

**3** *Saleem:* I'm Saleem Bashir. I'm from Kuala Lumpur, in Malaysia.

**1.3**  **Conversation 1**

*Saleem:* Hello. My name's Saleem Bashir. Here's my card.

*A:* Thank you. Where are you from?

*Saleem:* I'm from Malaysia.

*A:* Nice to meet you.

**Conversation 2**

*Alessandra:* Hello. My name's Alessandra Tivoli. Here's my card.

*B:* Thank you. Where are you from?

*Alessandra:* I'm from Italy.

*B:* Nice to meet you.

**Conversation 3**

*Sven:* Hello. My name's Sven Karlsson. Here's my card.

*C:* Thank you. Where are you from?

*Sven:* I'm from Sweden.

*C:* Nice to meet you.

**1.4**  I'm from Malaysia. // You're from Italy. // He's from France. // She's from Brazil. // We're from America. You're from Sweden. // They're from Poland.

### Unit 2  I'm a designer

**2.1**  *A:* Where's Fiona from?  |  *A:* What's her job?
*B:* She's from Scotland.  |  *B:* She's a designer.

**2.2**  Alessandra Tivoli is from Italy. She's a designer at Mimosa Cars.

Sven Karlsson is from Sweden. He's a sales manager at Splash Pools.

Saleem Bashir is from Malaysia. He's an engineer at KL Industries.

Astrid Schmidt is from Germany. She's a director at Supersport.

**2.3**  **1** an accountant   **2** a designer   **3** an engineer
**4** a lawyer   **5** a sales manager   **6** a personal assistant

**2.4**  *Alessandra:*
Hello. Welcome to Mimosa. My name's Alessandra and I'm a designer here at Mimosa Cars. I work in this office with Riccardo: his desk and his computer are over there. Don't touch them! You work here: your desk is here and your computer is over here.

**2.5**  **On the line**

*Melanie:* Is Alessandra Tivoli there?

*Alessandra:* Yes, speaking.

*Melanie:* Hello, Alessandra. This is Melanie.

*Alessandra:* Hello, Melanie …

### Unit 3  How many showrooms?

**3.1**  *A:* Are you from Argentina?
*B:* No, I'm not. I'm from Chile.

*A:* Is he from Australia?
*B:* No, he isn't. He's from New Zealand.

*A:* Is she from France?
*B:* No, she isn't. She's from Belgium.

*A:* Are you from Japan?
*B:* No, we aren't. We're from Korea.

*A:* Are they from Egypt?
*B:* No, they aren't. They're from Tunisia.

**3.2**  **1** *B:* There's an office in London.

**2** *A:* Is there an office in Manchester?
*B:* No, there isn't.

**3** *A:* Are there showrooms in Scotland?
*B:* No, there aren't.

**4** *A:* How many showrooms are there in England?
*B:* There are three showrooms.

**5** *A:* How many employees are there in Europe?
*B:* There are 120 employees.

**3.3**  zero, ten // one, eleven // two, twelve // twenty // three, thirteen, thirty // four, fourteen, forty // five, fifteen, fifty // six, sixteen, sixty // seven, seventeen, seventy // eight, eighteen, eighty // nine, nineteen, ninety // a hundred

**3.4** thirteen, fourteen, fifty // sixteen, seventy, eighty, nineteen, ninety // a hundred, a hundred and twenty-five, three hundred and thirty-three, three hundred and eighty-nine, four hundred and ninety-nine

**3.5** **On the line**

*Receptionist:* Hello.

*Carole:* Is that Splash Pools?

*Receptionist:* Yes, it is.

*Carole:* Can I speak to Sven Karlsson, please?

*Receptionist:* Who's calling?

## Unit 4  We make cars

**4.1** Saleem works for KL Industries.

He manages a car factory.

He lives in Kuala Lumpur.

He likes his job.

He loves cars.

**4.2** *Interviewer:* Do you speak English?
*Saleem:* Yes, I do.

*Interviewer:* Do you work in an office?
*Saleem:* Yes, I do.

*Interviewer:* Do you sell things?
*Saleem:* No, I don't.

*Interviewer:* Do you manage people?
*Saleem:* Yes, I do.

*Interviewer:* Do you like your job?
*Saleem:* Yes, I do!

**4.3** a  h  j  k // b  c  d  e  g  p  t  v // f  l  m
n  s  x  z // i  y // o // q  u  w // r

**4.4** **On the line**

**Conversation 1**

*PA:* Hello. Mr Bashir's personal assistant.

*Ray:* Hello. Can I speak to Mr Bashir, please?

*PA:* Who's calling?

*Ray:* This is Ray Baxter in New York.

*PA:* I'm sorry, but Mr Bashir isn't here today.

*Ray:* Can he call me tomorrow, please?

*PA:* How do you spell your name, please?

*Ray:* B-A-X ...

*PA:* B-A-X ...

*Ray:* T-E-R.

*PA:* T-A-R.

*Ray:* No. T-*E*-R.

*PA:* Oh, E, right.

*Ray:* My number's 001 ...

*PA:* 001 ...

*Ray:* 212 ...

*PA:* 212 ...

*Ray:* 734 ...

*PA:* 734 ...

*Ray:* 8923.

*PA:* 001 212 734 8923.

*Ray:* That's it. Thank you. Bye.

*PA:* Goodbye.

**Conversation 2**

*PA:* Mr Bashir's personal assistant.

*Paolo:* Hello. This is Paolo Ponte. Can I speak to Mr Bashir, please?

*PA:* I'm sorry, but he isn't here today.

*Paolo:* Can he send me an e-mail with details of his trip to Italy next week, please?

*PA:* What's your e-mail address?

*Paolo:* Paolo dot Ponte at Mimosa dot I-T ...

*PA:* Can you say that again?

*Paolo:* I'll spell it. P-A-O-L-O dot P-O-N-T-E.

*PA:* Paolo dot Ponte.

*Paolo:* At M-I-M-O-S-A dot I-T.

*PA:* At Mimosa dot I-T. OK. I'll tell him.

*Paolo:* Thank you very much. Bye.

*PA:* Goodbye.

## Unit 5  She goes to Spain

**5.1** *A:* Does he take a break in August?
*B:* No, he doesn't.

*A:* Does she go to Spain or Italy?
*B:* Yes, she does.

*A:* Does it leave at 10.15?
*B:* No, it doesn't.

He doesn't take a break in August. He takes a break in July.

She doesn't go to France. She goes to Spain or Italy.

It doesn't leave at 10.15. It leaves at 11.15.

**5.2** What time is it?

**a** It's eight thirty.
It's half past eight.

**b** It's eight forty-five.
It's a quarter to nine.

**c** It's nine o'clock.

**d** It's nine fifteen.
It's a quarter past nine.

**e** It's nine twenty-five.
It's twenty-five past nine.

**f** It's nine forty.
It's twenty to ten.

**g** It's ten o'clock.

**h** It's ten oh five.
It's five past ten.

**5.3  On the line**

**Conversation 1**

*Astrid:* Hello.

*Julia:* Astrid, hi. It's Julia.

*Astrid:* Where are you?

*Julia:* I'm at the hotel entrance, but there aren't any taxis.

*Astrid:* It's 9.15 now. The flight's at 10.30. I'm at the check-in desk at the airport.

*Julia:* Ah, here's a taxi. I'm on my way …

**Conversation 2**

*Astrid:* Hello.

*Julia:* Hi, Astrid. It's Julia.

*Astrid:* Where are you now?

*Julia:* Still about five kilometres from the airport. The traffic's very bad today.

*Astrid:* The flight's in 45 minutes, and they close the gate 15 minutes before the flight. The airport's very busy today. I'm at the café in the airport …

**Conversation 3**

*Astrid:* Hello.

*Julia:* It's me.

*Astrid:* Where are you?

*Julia:* I'm two kilometres from the airport. The traffic's still terrible. It's five past ten. You get on the plane. There's another flight this afternoon. I'll see you in Innsbruck this evening.

*Astrid:* OK. I'm at the departure gate.

*Announcement:* Lufthansa announces the departure of flight LH 392 to Innsbruck. Will all passengers …

*Astrid:* That's our flight! I'll see you at the hotel later.

*Julia:* What's the name of the hotel?

*Astrid:* The Palace. See you there.

*Julia:* OK. See you at the Palace Hotel this evening. Bye for now.

*Astrid:* Bye.

# Unit 6  How do you relax?

**6.1**  *Interviewer:* Excuse me, sir. Can I ask you some questions?

*John:* Sure.

*Interviewer:* What's your name?

*John:* John Baker.

*Interviewer:* Where do you live?

*John:* I live right here in Sacramento.

*Interviewer:* Do you play any of these sports: soccer, hockey or baseball?

*John:* Yeah, I play soccer with my friends in the park on the weekend.

*Interviewer:* And hockey?

*John:* No, I don't play hockey.

*Interviewer:* What about baseball?

*John:* I don't play baseball, but I watch it on TV when there's a big game. My friends come to the house and we have a few beers.

*Interviewer:* And do you go walking, camping or skiing?

*John:* Yes, I go skiing with my son at Lake Tahoe on the weekend and I go camping with him too. My wife stays home.

*Interviewer:* How old is your son?

*John:* Twelve.

*Interviewer:* And what's his name?

*John:* Jason – Jason Baker.

*Interviewer:* And where do you go camping?

*John:* We go to the Rocky Mountains. My son loves it there.

*Interviewer:* And what sports does he play?

*John:* He plays soccer with his friends at school in the evening, but he doesn't play baseball or hockey.

*Interviewer:* Thank you very much for your time.

*John:* Sure.

**6.2**  1  How do you relax?

2  When do you play football?

3  Where do you play?

4  Who do you play with?

5  How often do you win?

6  Why do you play football and not hockey?

**6.3**  1  *Interviewer:* How do you relax?
  *Boy:* I play football.

2  *Interviewer:* When do you play football?
  *Boy:* At the weekend.

3  *Interviewer:* Where do you play?
  *Boy:* In the park.

4  *Interviewer:* Who do you play with?
  *Boy:* With friends.

5  *Interviewer:* How often do you win?
  *Boy:* Not every time!

6  *Interviewer:* Why do you play football and not hockey?
  *Boy:* Because it's more exciting!

**6.4  On the line**

*Receptionist:* Magic World Park. How can I help?

*Man:* Hello. What time does the park open today?

*Receptionist:* 10 am.

*Man:* And what time does it close?

*Receptionist:* 9 pm.

*Man:* And the restaurant?

*Receptionist:* It opens at 11.30 am, and they serve the last meal at 8 pm.

| | |
|---|---|
| Man: | And when does the first Ghost train leave? |
| Receptionist: | The first one leaves at 10.30 am and the last one leaves at 6.30 pm. |
| Man: | This is my last question. What time does the cinema open and what time does it close? |
| Receptionist: | The first film show is at 2.30 pm and the last film show is at 7.15 pm. |
| Man: | Thank you very much. |
| Receptionist: | You're welcome. |

## Review 1–6

**R1.1**  **1** Varig announces the departure of flight RG 993 to Rio, gate number 44.

**2** Alitalia announces the departure of flight AZ 728 to Rome, gate number 12.

**3** Virgin announces the depature of flight VS 223 to London, gate number 9.

**4** Northwest announces the departure of flight NW 616 to Los Angeles, gate number 26.

**5** South African Airways announces the departure of flight SA 821 to Cape Town, gate number 31.

**6** Air Jamaica announces the departure of flight JM 832 to Kingston, gate number 17.

# Module 2  Splash Pools

## Unit 7  We get a lot of visitors

**7.1**  **On the line**

| | |
|---|---|
| Receptionist: | Splash Pools, good morning. |
| Carole: | Hello. Can I speak to someone in sales, please? |
| Receptionist: | Who's calling, please? |
| Carole: | Carole Bruckner of Energy Gyms. |
| Receptionist: | One moment. |
| Sven: | Karlsson. |
| Carole: | Hi, my name's Carole Bruckner. I work for Energy Gyms here in the UK. Do you know Energy Gyms? |
| Sven: | Of course. How can I help you? |
| Carole: | We have plans to open a lot of gyms in the UK in the next year or two, and we want to buy saunas for our new gyms. |
| Sven: | Right. |
| Carole: | Can I come to talk about it at your showroom? |
| Sven: | Yes, no problem. How about Thursday this week? |
| Carole: | I'm busy on Thursday. How about Friday morning? 11 o'clock? |
| Sven: | Fine. |
| Carole: | What's the address? |

| | |
|---|---|
| Sven: | There's a map with the address and directions on how to get here on our website: www dot splashpools dot co dot uk. |
| Carole: | OK. See you Friday at 11. |
| Sven: | See you then. Bye for now. |

## Unit 8  Turn left at the lights

**8.1**  **On the line**

| | |
|---|---|
| Receptionist: | Splash Pools, good morning. |
| Carole: | Hello. I'm trying to find your showroom and I'm lost. Where *is* your showroom? |
| Receptionist: | Where are you? |
| Carole: | I'm not sure. Ah, here's a sign 'Stockwell Road'. |
| Receptionist: | OK. Go along Stockwell Road towards Stockwell tube and turn left into Clapham Road. |
| Carole: | Clapham Road, OK. |
| Receptionist: | At Clapham North station, go straight on into Clapham High Street. The Splash Pools showroom is on the left, opposite Stonehouse Street. |
| Carole: | Clapham High Street, opposite Stonehouse Street. |
| Receptionist: | You can't miss it. |
| Carole: | OK. Oh, I have a meeting with Sven Karlsson. Can you tell him I'll be late? My name's Carole Bruckner. |
| Receptionist: | OK, I'll do that, Ms Bruckner. |
| Carole: | Thanks. Bye. |
| Receptionist: | Bye. |

**8.2**  **Conversation 1**

A: Tea?

B: Yes, please.

A: Sugar?

B: Two, please.

A: Here you are.

B: Thanks.

**Conversation 2**

C: Would you like a coffee?

D: Yes, please.

C: How do you like it?

D: White, one sugar, please.

C: Here you are.

D: Thanks.

**Conversation 3**

E: Would you like some juice?

F: No, thanks.

E: Sure?

F: I'm OK, thanks.

**8.3**

**Carole:** Hello. My name's Carole Bruckner. I have a meeting with Sven Karlsson.

**Receptionist:** I'll call him. Sven, hi. Ms Bruckner is here to see you ... OK, I'll tell her. He's coming down now ...

**Sven:** Hello, I'm Sven Karlsson.

**Carole:** Carole Bruckner. Pleased to meet you, Mr Karlsson. Sorry I'm late – there's a lot of traffic today.

**Sven:** That's all right. Let's go up to my office ...

**Carole:** Right ...

**Sven:** This is my office. Have a seat. Would you like some tea, coffee or juice?

**Carole:** Black coffee with sugar, please ... Thanks.

**Sven:** Tell me something about your company.

**Carole:** Energy Gyms is an American company, of course. We have seven gyms in the UK, with plans to open ten more in the next two years.

**Sven:** Right ...

**Carole:** And we want to buy saunas and Jacuzzis for all our new gyms.

**Sven:** Interesting ...

## Unit 9  Can I help you?

**9.1** Can I help you?

You can't smoke in here.

When can you deliver?

Can you send a brochure?

We can't deliver before next year.

**9.2** **On the line**

**Sven:** Karlsson.

**Carole:** Hello, Sven – it's Carole Bruckner. How are you today?

**Sven:** Fine. Good game of golf yesterday! And you? Good weekend?

**Carole:** Very good, thanks. I'm calling to place our order for the saunas.

**Sven:** Good!

**Carole:** We want twenty indoor saunas, ten next month and ten the month after. Can you do that?

**Sven:** No problem.

**Carole:** You have them in white and blue, right?

**Sven:** Yes.

**Carole:** Good. We'll have ten blue ones next month, and ten white ones the month after.

**Sven:** OK. No problem at all.

**Carole:** And the price. The basic price is £5,000 each and you're giving us a 12 per cent discount, aren't you?

**Sven:** 10 per cent is our normal discount. But we can give 12 per cent just for you!

**Carole:** Good. I'll send you an e-mail today with our order. What's your e-mail address?

**Sven:** Sven dot Karlsson at splashpools dot co dot uk.

**Carole:** Sven dot Karlsson ...

**Sven:** Karlsson with a K and two Ss.

**Carole:** At splashpools dot co dot uk – splashpools all one word, right?

**Sven:** That's it. So, thank you very much for your order.

**Carole:** It's good to do business with you! Bye for now!

**Sven:** Bye.

## Unit 10  I'm buying a house

**10.1** I'm planning the garden now.

You're planning the garden now.

He's planning the garden now.

She's planning the garden now.

We're planning the garden now.

You're planning the garden now.

They're planning the garden now.

*A:* Is she looking for a sauna?

*B:* No, she isn't looking for a sauna. She's looking for a Jacuzzi.

*A:* Are you hoping to buy it soon?

*B:* Yes, we are. We're hoping to buy it this week.

*A:* Are they moving into the house today?

*B:* No, they aren't.

**10.2** **Sven:** We have an enquiry about a Jacuzzi from a customer – her name's er ... Teresa Pym. Can you deal with it, Tania?

**Tania:** Is she spending a lot with us?

**Sven:** No, she only wants a Jacuzzi – she's only spending about five thousand pounds.

**Tania:** No – sorry, Sven. I'm busy. I'm working on another order at the moment.

**Sven:** What's that?

**Tania:** I'm working on a big order for Brilliant Gyms. They're spending three hundred thousand pounds.

**Sven:** Oh, right. Where are the other salespeople? What's Len doing?

**Tania:** He's visiting a customer.

**Sven:** And Cathy?

**Tania:** She's making coffee.

**Sven:** What, again? She drinks too much coffee! And where's Brian?

**Tania:** He's on holiday.

**Sven:** Oh, right. I remember now.

**Tania:** He's probably swimming in the Mediterranean right now – lucky guy!

**Sven:** Yes, he's very lucky ... OK, I can work on the order for Teresa Pym myself ...

## 10.3 On the line

Receptionist: Hello.

Joan: Hello. Is that Splash Pools?

Receptionist: Yes, it is.

Joan: Can I speak to Sven Karlsson, please?

Receptionist: Who's calling, please?

Joan: My name's Joan Smythe. I'm phoning from the Supreme Sports Club.

Receptionist: Unfortunately he's visiting a customer today.

Joan: Can you give him a message?

Receptionist: Of course.

Joan: I'm phoning about a meeting that we have tomorrow at 11 – I can't make it. Can you ask him to call me back?

Receptionist: Of course. Can you spell your name, please?

Joan: S-M-Y-T-H-E.

Receptionist: Does he have your number?

Joan: It's 020 …

Receptionist: 020 …

Joan: 9831 …

Receptionist: 9831 …

Joan: 3472.

Receptionist: 3472. OK, Ms Smythe, I'll give him the message.

Joan: Thanks, bye.

Receptionist: Goodbye.

# Unit 11 What's Sven doing?

## 11.1 On the line

Tracey: Hi, Sven. It's Tracey.

Sven: Hello, Tracey.

Tracey: Where are you?

Sven: I'm playing golf with a customer … and I'm winning!

Tracey: There's an e-mail from Carole Bruckner at Energy Gyms.

Sven: What does she want?

Tracey: She wants to know about her order. She's waiting for the delivery of her saunas. She wants to know where they are.

Sven: But it's Friday afternoon!

Tracey: She says it's very urgent.

Sven: Can you phone Carole? You have her number, I think.

Tracey: Yes, I have it.

Sven: Tell her that I'm out of the office visiting another customer.

Tracey: Right.

Sven: But tell her that I know about the problem. Tell her that I'm checking the delivery situation by phone. She can call me on Monday at the showroom if she wants.

Tracey: OK. Good luck with the golf!

Sven: Thanks. Have a good weekend!

Tracey: You too. See you on Monday morning.

Sven: Bye.

Tracey: Bye.

## 11.2
A: What's Sven doing?

B: He's playing golf.

A: Where's he playing?

B: At a golf club near London.

A: When's he playing?

B: On Friday afternoon.

A: Who's he playing?

B: A customer.

A: Why's he playing?

B: He wants an order.

A: How's he playing?

B: Very well. He's winning.

## 11.3
the first of May, May the first

the second of May, May the second

the third of May, May the third

the fourth of May, May the fourth

the fifth of May, May the fifth

the corner of Sixth Avenue and 42nd Street

second floor, third floor

# Unit 12 The truck's leaving now

## 12.1 On the line

Sven: Karlsson.

Carole: Hi, Sven. This is Carole Bruckner.

Sven: Hello, Carole – how are you?

Carole: Fine. Sven, I'm calling about our saunas. Delivery is this week, right?

Sven: I'm checking on the computer.

Carole: OK.

Sven: I have your order in front of me now. Ten blue Swedesaunas for the twenty-ninth of October – last week – and ten white ones for the end of November.

Carole: That's right. Can you tell me about delivery of the blue saunas? Where are they?

Sven: I'm sorry, but there are problems with delivery to us from the manufacturers in Sweden.

Carole: Oh …

Sven: The truck's leaving Gothenburg with your saunas today.

Carole: When's it arriving in the UK?

Sven: Tomorrow.

Carole: Oh …

Sven: We're very sorry about this late delivery.

Carole: OK. Can I call you tomorrow to check the situation?

*Sven:* Of course. Talk to you then. And our apologies for the delay.

*Carole:* That's all right. Bye for now.

*Sven:* Bye.

# Module 3  Macpherson Designs

## Unit 13  I work from home

**13.1** I try to work regular hours, from 8 to 5.30. But when there's a lot to do, I sometimes work in the evenings. For lunch, I have a sandwich.

In France, people in companies usually start work at 8.30 or 9. They finish at 5.30 or 6. They work 35 hours a week, but managers usually work longer. Lunch is very important and there's a long lunch break. I never phone people in companies in France between 12 and 2.30.

Here, the shops close at 1. They open again at about 4. Then they stay open quite late, until 7 or 8.

**13.2  On the line**

*Voice:* Thank you for calling the Cross Channel Ferry Company. Sorry to keep you waiting.

*Cheryl:* Cheryl speaking. How can I help?

*Douglas:* Hello. I want to book on the Dover–Calais service – two o'clock in the afternoon from Dover on the tenth of June.

*Cheryl:* Two o'clock, Sunday the tenth of June. What sort of car do you have?

*Douglas:* A Renault Laguna. Do you want the number?

*Cheryl:* Yes, please.

*Douglas:* X168 SNT.

*Cheryl:* X ... 168 ... I'm sorry, can you say the last three letters again?

*Douglas:* S for Sugar, N for November, T for Tango.

*Cheryl:* X ... 168 ... SNT ...  How many people are travelling?

*Douglas:* Two adults and two children, aged 10 and 13.

*Cheryl:* Can I have your name please?

*Douglas:* Macpherson: M-A-C-P-H-E-R-S-O-N.

*Cheryl:* And your first name, Mr Macpherson?

*Douglas:* Douglas.

*Cheryl:* Two adults, two children, one car, that's £254. How do you want to pay?

*Douglas:* Visa.

*Cheryl:* What's the number?

*Douglas:* 1068 ...

*Cheryl:* 1068 ...

*Douglas:* 4599 ...

*Cheryl:* 4599 ...

*Douglas:* 3427 ...

*Cheryl:* 3427 ...

*Douglas:* 2846.

*Cheryl:* 2846. Thanks.

**13.3  On the line**

*Cheryl:* So, to check the details. Your surname is Macpherson: M-A-C-P-H-E-R-S-O-N.

*Douglas:* That's right.

*Cheryl:* You're travelling with a Renault Laguna – two adults, two children, on the 10th of June at 2 pm.

*Douglas:* Right.

*Cheryl:* The number of the car is X168 SNT.

*Douglas:* Correct.

*Cheryl:* And you're paying by Visa, card number 1068 ...

## Unit 14  We're arriving on Monday

**14.1** *Fiona:* Hello.

*Douglas:* Hi, Fiona – this is Douglas.

*Fiona:* Hello, Douglas. When are you coming to see us?

*Douglas:* We're getting the ferry from Dover to Calais on Sunday.

*Fiona:* You're driving from Aberdeen to Dover in one go!?

*Douglas:* No. We're staying at a hotel in York on Saturday evening and at a hotel in Versailles on Sunday evening.

*Fiona:* Oh, right.

*Douglas:* We're arriving at your house at about 8 o'clock on Monday evening. Is that OK?

*Fiona:* In my diary, I have Tuesday evening!

*Douglas:* No, we're arriving on Monday evening!

*Fiona:* OK. No problem. It's about ten hours by car from Versailles to here.

*Douglas:* We're looking forward to seeing you.

*Fiona:* Have a good journey!

*Douglas:* See you Monday. Bye for now.

*Fiona:* Bye.

**14.2** *Douglas:* What are you doing on Monday next week?

*Fiona:* In the morning and the afternoon, I'm working on a design project for a company called Sigma. And in the evening you're arriving.

*Douglas:* What are you doing on Tuesday?

*Fiona:* In the morning I'm finishing the Sigma project, and in the afternoon I'm free, so we can do something together.

*Douglas:* What about Wednesday?

*Fiona:* In the morning I'm working on a project for a company called Noval.

*Douglas:* And in the afternoon?

*Fiona:* I'm meeting someone at the tourist office in Biarritz ...

**14.3** man   men // woman   women // child   children // person   people // family   families // diary   diaries // box   boxes // watch   watches

**14.4  On the line**

*Receptionist:*  Hotel du Parc, bonjour.

*Douglas:*  Hello. I'd like to make a reservation, please.

*Receptionist:*  Of course. For what date?

*Douglas:*  Sunday the tenth of June.

*Receptionist:*  How many nights are you staying?

*Douglas:*  Just one.

*Receptionist:*  For how many people?

*Douglas:*  Two adults – my wife and myself – and two children – two boys aged 10 and 13.

*Receptionist:*  So you want two rooms, right?

*Douglas:*  Yes, please. One for my wife and myself and one for the children.

*Receptionist:*  OK. The price per room is 120 euros. Can you give me your name and your credit card number?

*Douglas:*  Right. My name's Douglas Macpherson: M-A-C-P-H-E-R-S-O-N. And my card number is 4408 …

*Receptionist:*  4408.

*Douglas:*  0412 …

*Receptionist:*  0412.

*Douglas:*  3456 …

*Receptionist:*  3456.

*Douglas:*  7890 …

*Receptionist:*  7890. What time are you arriving?

*Douglas:*  About 8 pm.

*Receptionist:*  OK. So that's two rooms for the night of Sunday the tenth of June at 120 euros each in the name of Macpherson, and you're arriving about 8 pm.

*Douglas:*  That's right. Thank you very much. Bye.

*Receptionist:*  Goodbye.

## Unit 15  Can we order, please?

**15.1  Conversation 1a**

*Douglas:*  Good evening. I have a reservation in the name of Macpherson.

*Receptionist:*  I'm sorry, sir, but the hotel's closed. There's a problem with the electricity.

*Douglas:*  Oh, no! Is there another hotel near here?

*Receptionist:*  Yes, please could you go to the Hotel Excelsior – 200 metres down the road. They have rooms …

**Conversation 1b**

*Douglas:*  I have a reservation – name of Macpherson.

*Receptionist:*  The hotel's closed. No electricity.

*Douglas:*  Oh, no! Is there another hotel near here?

*Receptionist:*  Excelsior – 200 metres down the road. They have rooms …

**Conversation 2a**

*Douglas:*  Hello. Where do we get the 2 o'clock ferry to Calais, please?

*Ferry man:*  The 2 o'clock to Calais? I'm sorry, but it's cancelled because of bad weather. Can you wait over there, please?

*Douglas:*  OK. Thanks …

**Conversation 2b**

*Douglas:*  Where do we get the 2 o'clock to Calais?

*Ferry man:*  The two o'clock to Calais? It's cancelled. Wait over there.

*Douglas:*  OK …

**Conversation 3a**

*Douglas:*  Good evening. Can we have a table for four, please?

*Waiter:*  Do you have a reservation?

*Douglas:*  No, we don't.

*Waiter:*  I'm sorry, but we're full. We're very busy. You could try our other restaurant – 23 rue Mazarin.

*Douglas:*  OK. Thank you …

**Conversation 3b**

*Douglas:*  Give us a table for four.

*Waiter:*  Do you have a reservation?

*Douglas:*  No.

*Waiter:*  We're full. We're very busy. Go to our other restaurant – 23 rue Mazarin.

*Douglas:*  OK …

**15.2  On the line**

*Fiona:*  Hello.

*Douglas:*  Fiona, hi – it's Douglas.

*Fiona:*  Where are you?

*Douglas:*  We're leaving Versailles. We're driving south on the motorway.

*Fiona:*  How's the trip going?

*Douglas:*  The hotel in York was closed, the ferry from Dover to Calais was cancelled, and the restaurant in Versailles wasn't very good. In fact, the food was terrible!

*Fiona:*  Oh, no …

*Douglas:*  But the hotel in Versailles was very comfortable.

*Fiona:*  Good.

*Douglas:*  I'll tell you more this evening.

*Fiona:*  OK. See you this evening. Have a good journey. Bye.

*Douglas:*  Bye for now.

## Unit 16  I decided to move to France

**16.1**  like   liked // move   moved // decide   decided // need   needed // buy   bought // do   did // have   had // go   went

**16.2**  **1**  Fiona grew up on Skye, but she didn't stay there.

**2**  She studied in Glasgow. She didn't want to go to London.

**3** Fiona got a job at a design company, but she didn't like her boss.

**4** Then she worked from home for four years, but she didn't feel lonely.

**5** She bought a house in the south-west of France. She didn't move to Paris.

**16.3** **1** *A:* Did she grow up on the Isle of Skye?

*B:* Yes, she did.

**2** *A:* Did she go to a design school in Glasgow?

*B:* Yes, she did.

**3** *A:* Did she work from home for four years?

*B:* Yes, she did.

**4** *A:* Did she move to a big city in France?

*B:* No, she didn't. She moved to a small village.

**5** *A:* Did she buy a house in the Alps?

*B:* No, she didn't. She bought a house in the Pyrenees.

**6** *A:* Did she know the Pyrenees before she moved there?

*B:* Yes, she did.

**16.4** *Douglas:* We're here!

*Fiona:* Hi! Come in. Hi Sandra, hello kids. Did you find the house OK?

*Sandra:* No problem.

*Fiona:* Good. Did you have a good journey?

*Douglas:* When we phoned from the motorway near Versailles, the traffic really was terrible, but after Versailles it was a very easy journey.

*Fiona:* Did you stop for lunch in a restaurant?

*Sandra:* No, we had a sandwich at a service station on the motorway. We didn't want to leave the motorway and lose time.

*Fiona:* Did you bring a lot of luggage?

*Douglas:* No, not a lot. Only one small bag each. We can get them from the car now …

# Unit 17 Did you get my message?

**17.1** **Message 1**

*Michelle:*

Michelle Dulac here, at the Biarritz tourist office, about our meeting on Wednesday. I have a problem with Wednesday afternoon. Can you call me back so we can fix another time? Thank you.

**Message 2**

*Magali:*

It's Magali Martin at Midi Editions. I'm phoning about the designs that you agreed to send us. We wanted them by Wednesday last week. It's now Tuesday afternoon. I sent you e-mails, but you didn't answer them. I sent you a letter on Friday. Did you get that? Please call me as soon as possible.

**Message 3**

*Jacques:*

This is Jacques Lebrun at Sigma in Paris. I got your e-mail with the package design – it looks great! But there are one or two things that I'd like to talk about. Can you contact me tomorrow, Wednesday? Bye.

**Message 4**

*Amanda:*

Hello, it's Amanda Lee-Smith at Pocket Books. The cover design project we talked about is now very urgent. We want something by next week if possible. Can you give me a call to talk about things? Thanks.

**17.2** **On the line**

*Magali:* Allo.

*Fiona:* Can I speak to Magali Martin, please?

*Magali:* Speaking.

*Fiona:* This is Fiona Macpherson.

*Magali:* Right. Did you get my letter? Did you get my message on your answering machine?

*Fiona:* I got your letter and your phone message when I came in yesterday evening.

*Magali:* Did you get my e-mails last week? I sent one on Thursday and one on Friday.

*Fiona:* I got your letter and phone message, but I didn't get any e-mails. I think there was a problem with my computer.

*Magali:* Anyway, where are our designs?

*Fiona:* Actually, I'm having problems with them. I have one or two ideas, but I need more time.

*Magali:* Mmm.

*Fiona:* I'm sorry about this. Can you give me two or three more days?

*Magali:* This is very urgent now. Could you send something on Friday?

*Fiona:* How about Monday? I can work on the designs during the weekend.

*Magali:* OK, please can you send them on Monday. We really need them by Tuesday morning.

*Fiona:* Thank you. I'm sorry about this delay.

*Magali:* OK. I'm looking forward to getting them on Tuesday. Goodbye.

*Fiona:* Bye.

# Unit 18 Where did you go?

**18.1** *Magali:* Hello, Fiona – good to see you. How was the trip?

*Fiona:* Not too bad.

*Magali:* Did you get the train?

*Fiona:* No, I drove.

*Magali:* How long did it take?

*Fiona:* Two and a half hours. The motorway wasn't very busy.

*Magali:* Would you like some coffee?

*Fiona:* No, thanks. I drink too much coffee – it's one of the problems when you work at home. Do you have some juice?

*Magali:* Juice – no problem. Here you are.

*Fiona:* Thanks.

*Magali:* As I said on the phone, I got the designs for the cover of *The Wonderful Pyrenees* book on Tuesday.

*Fiona:* Right.

*Magali:* I like the photos in the design a lot. Pictures of Biarritz – very good idea! Where did you get them?

*Fiona:* I took them myself.

*Magali:* Really!? So you're not only a designer. You're a photographer too!

*Fiona:* That's right.

*Magali:* Are you interested in taking photos for the whole book?

*Fiona* Yes, of course!

**18.2** **1** *Douglas:* Where did you go yesterday?
*Fiona:* I went to Toulouse.

**2** *Douglas:* How did you get there?
*Fiona:* I drove.

**3** *Douglas:* Who did you see?
*Fiona:* Magali Martin at Midi Editions.

**4** *Douglas:* Why did you see her?
*Fiona:* To talk about a book on the Pyrenees.

**5** *Douglas:* How long did the meeting take?
*Fiona:* About two hours.

**6** *Douglas:* What did you agree?
*Fiona:* I agreed to take the photos for the book.

**18.3** **On the line**
*Fiona:* Hello. Fiona Macpherson.

*Magali:* Hello, Fiona. This is Magali. Did you get my e-mail OK?

*Fiona:* Yes. But I don't agree with one or two things in it. They're not what we decided when I came to see you.

*Magali:* Aren't they?

*Fiona:* Well, for example, I thought the title of the book was *The Wonderful Pyrenees,* but in your e-mail you put *The Beautiful Pyrenees.*

*Magali:* That's a mistake. It's *The Wonderful Pyrenees.*

*Fiona:* And in the e-mail you say that I'm writing the text, but at the meeting we didn't talk about the text – I thought someone else was writing the text.

*Magali:* No, I'm sure at the meeting we talked about you writing the text.

*Fiona:* That's not what I wrote in my notes. Another thing – we decided on delivery of the cover

design in two months and in the e-mail it says one month.

*Magali:* No. I'm sure at the meeting we said one month.

*Fiona:* I wrote two months in the notes I took. And for the photos, we decided on delivery in five months, not three months.

*Magali:* OK, I'll send you an e-mail to confirm all these points …

## Module 4  Supersport

## Unit 19  Supersport has arrived

**19.1** arrive   arrived **//** invest   invested **//** move   moved build   built **//** make   made **//** sell   sold

**19.2** **On the line**
This is Supersport's New York office. For the accounts department, press one. For the human resources department, press two. For the planning department, press three. For Astrid Schmidt's office, press four. For all other enquiries, please hold.

## Unit 20  Do you have any tents?

**20.1** **Conversation 1**
*Customer:* Hi. I'm calling about bikes. Do you have any Armstrong bikes in stock?

*Salesperson:* Yes, we do. We have three or four in stock.

*Customer:* And what about the Lemond model? Do you have any of those at the moment?

*Salesperson:* No, we don't. We're out of stock …

**Conversation 2**
*Customer:* Hello. Do you have any Alamo tents at the moment?

*Salesperson:* No, we don't. We're expecting some next week.

*Customer:* And Bute tents. Do you have any of those?

*Salesperson:* Yes, I think we have about ten in stock …

**Conversation 3**
*Customer:* Hi. I want to come in and buy an X500 jacket. Do you have any in stock?

*Salesperson:* Yes, we have some here right now, but we're out of the X600s.

*Customer:* OK …

**Conversation 4**
*Customer:* Hi. I'm going to the Rocky Mountains next week. I need some new boots.

*Salesperson:* OK. We have some very good Austrian and Italian boots at the moment.

*Customer:* Great. I'll come in and try them …

### Conversation 5

*Customer:* Hello. I'm going to South America. Do you have any maps of Colombia and Ecuador?

*Salesperson:* Well, we have maps of Ecuador. But we're expecting maps of Colombia to come in next week.

*Customer:* I'm leaving on Saturday. I'll try somewhere else. Thanks anyway.

*Salesperson:* No problem …

**20.2** We have some maps of Ecuador. // We have some Austrian boots. // We don't have any Italian boots. // There aren't any Alamo tents. // Do you have any X500 jackets? // Are there any American boots in stock? // Would you like some coffee?

**20.3 On the line**

### Conversation 1

*Salesperson:* Bike department, may I help you?

*Customer:* Hi. I'm calling about bikes. Do you have any Simpson bikes in stock?

*Salesperson:* We have some Simpson bikes, but we don't have any Anquetil bikes. We have eight Simpsons in stock.

*Customer:* OK, can I come in and look at the Simpson bikes this evening?

*Salesperson:* Of course.

*Customer:* What time do you close?

*Salesperson:* At 9 pm.

*Customer:* Thanks for your help.

*Salesperson:* Sure …

### Conversation 2

*Salesperson:* Tent department, how may I help you?

*Customer:* Hello. Do you have any McKinley tents at the moment?

*Salesperson:* No, we don't have any in stock. We're expecting some next week.

*Customer:* And what about Ogden tents. Do you have any of those?

*Salesperson:* Yes, I think we have one left.

*Customer:* Can you keep it for me until tomorrow afternoon, around 5 pm. Is that OK?

*Salesperson:* Sure …

### Conversation 3

*Salesperson:* Clothing, how may I help you?

*Customer:* Hi. I want to come in and buy an X400 jacket. Do you have any in stock?

*Salesperson:* Yes, we have some here – about twelve, I think. But we don't have any X300s. What size do you take?

*Customer:* XL – Extra large.

*Salesperson:* Yes, we have some extra large ones.

*Customer:* I'll come in tomorrow and try one.

*Salesperson:* Fine. It's my day off tomorrow, but you can talk to my colleague.

*Customer:* OK. Thanks …

### Conversation 4

*Salesperson:* Map department, may I help you?

*Customer:* Hello. I'm going to South America soon. Do you have any maps of Brazil and Peru?

*Salesperson:* Well, we have some maps of Brazil – about twenty of different parts of the country. But we don't have any maps of Peru – we're expecting them next week.

*Customer:* I'm leaving on Saturday. I know another place where I can get them. Thanks anyway.

*Salesperson:* No problem …

## Unit 21  The service was slow

**21.1 Interview 1**

*Interviewer:* Excuse me. I see you bought a tent. How much did you pay for it?

*Customer:* $799. Much cheaper than at the other store I went to this morning, where the same tent costs $999! That's a great deal!

*Interviewer:* And what did you think of the service?

*Customer:* The salespeople were unfriendly.

*Interviewer:* Thank you.

**Interview 2**

*Interviewer:* Excuse me, ma'am. What did you buy?

*Customer:* We're going on a skiing trip soon, so I bought skis for my children.

*Interviewer:* How much did you pay?

*Customer:* Each pair of skis was $200. I bought three pairs, so I paid $600 in all.

*Interviewer:* What did you think of the service?

*Customer:* Very helpful. The saleswoman answered all my questions. And she's carrying the skis to my car for me right now! I'm certainly coming back here again!

**Interview 3**

*Interviewer:* What did you buy?

*Customer:* I came here for a jacket, but in the end I didn't buy anything.

*Interviewer:* Was the service good?

*Customer:* No, it was very slow. I wanted to ask some questions but no one came to help me.

**Interview 4**

*Interviewer:* What did you get, sir?

*Customer:* I play soccer, and I wanted to buy some soccer shoes.

*Interviewer:* What did you think of the service?

*Customer:* The salesman was very friendly but they didn't have any in stock – not my size anyway. I'm going to look somewhere else – I'm going to the Sportmart store.

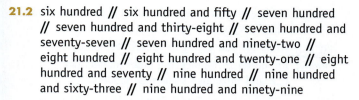

**21.2** six hundred // six hundred and fifty // seven hundred // seven hundred and thirty-eight // seven hundred and seventy-seven // seven hundred and ninety-two // eight hundred // eight hundred and twenty-one // eight hundred and seventy // nine hundred // nine hundred and sixty-three // nine hundred and ninety-nine

**21.3 On the line**

*Lola:* Fernandez.

*Harry:* Hi, Lola – it's Harry at Supersport.

*Lola:* Hi, Harry. How are you today?

*Harry:* Good. Thanks for your e-mail with the report.

*Lola:* Sure.

*Harry:* There's a problem with the attachment and some of the figures are missing. Can I check them with you?

*Lola:* Sure. Just a moment.

*Harry:* The first line – quality of products – is OK. But in the second line – choice of products – what are the figures?

*Lola:* Choice of products: 40 per cent of customers think the choice of products is excellent, 33 per cent good, 17 per cent fair, 10 per cent poor.

*Harry:* Excellent 40, good 33, fair 17, poor 10. And the next line, availability of products?

*Lola:* Availability of products: excellent 9, good 18, fair 44, poor 29.

*Harry:* Excellent 9, good 18 ...

## Unit 22  The smallest company

**22.1**

| a thousand | a million | 7 billion |
|---|---|---|
| 93,000 | 5 million dollars | 21 billion dollars |
| 800,000 euros | 70 million | 87 billion |
| | 278 million | 500 billion dollars |

## Unit 23  You must improve training

**23.1 On the line**

*Harry:* Esposito.

*Astrid:* This is Astrid Schmidt in New York.

*Harry:* Hi, Astrid.

*Astrid:* How's it going today?

*Harry:* Good. The store is busier than last week.

*Astrid:* Right. But I think there are some big problems. The sales are lower than we wanted.

*Harry:* Yes, I know.

*Astrid:* I'd like to come and see things in Sacramento for myself next week. Is Tuesday OK?

*Harry:* Yes, of course.

*Astrid:* I can get the early flight from New York. I'll get a taxi from the airport and I'll be with you around 12.

*Harry:* OK.

*Astrid:* I want to spend two or three days in the store talking to salespeople and customers.

*Harry:* Right.

*Astrid:* So can you ask your PA to reserve a hotel for two nights – Tuesday night and Wednesday night? Somewhere in the centre of Sacramento?

*Harry:* A hotel for two nights in the centre, OK. I'll ask my PA to do that.

*Astrid:* Thanks, Harry. See you on Tuesday. Bye for now.

*Harry:* Bye.

**23.2** *Astrid:* I've read the report. Things aren't going well.

*Harry:* I know. But the store's busier this week.

*Astrid:* Yes, but are the people in the store buying our products?

*Harry:* Well, we have good products – customers think that the products are excellent.

*Astrid:* But you don't order the products on time.

*Harry:* The problem isn't here in Sacramento. It's the central computer in New York.

*Astrid:* We must improve the system.

*Harry:* OK. Another problem is the salespeople.

*Astrid:* I know. Customers aren't happy with the service.

*Harry:* Yes, but it's difficult to find staff who know about sporting goods. We must increase pay and find better people.

*Astrid:* I don't agree. I think we must train the staff that we have ...

## Unit 24  Follow my advice

**24.1 On the line**

*Astrid:* Astrid Schmidt.

*Jim:* Hello, Astrid. It's Jim. You asked me to call you.

*Astrid:* Yes, I did. Jim, I visited our new store in Sacramento yesterday.

*Jim:* How's it going there?

*Astrid:* The store manager says there's a problem with the computer system. Customers come into the store and they ask for goods that aren't in stock.

*Jim:* Right. I think the real problem is that the salespeople there don't know how to use the computer system. I think they need ...

*Astrid:* Jim, I have a suggestion.

*Jim:* Yes.

*Astrid:* I want you to go to Sacramento for three months to train the staff to use the computer system.

*Jim:* Mmm. Interesting idea ...

*Astrid:* Can you come and see me so we can discuss it in more detail?

*Jim:* Of course.

*Astrid:* How about tomorrow afternoon at 2?

*Jim:* OK. See you then. Bye.

*Astrid:* Bye.

# Module 5  Mimosa Cars

## Unit 25  Don't drive too fast!

### 25.1  On the line

#### Message 1

*Jong-Hun:* This is Jong-Hun Park from Hyundai in Seoul. You remember we met at the International Car Design Conference in Madrid last week. I'm in Paris at the moment but I'm visiting Modena on Tuesday. Would you like to meet for lunch? Give me a call on 00 33 1 78 32 45 61. Thanks. Hope to see you on Tuesday.

#### Message 2

*Ray:* My name's Ray Baxter, from *World Sports Car News*. I don't know if you saw my article about Mimosa in the magazine. I wanted to talk to a designer at Mimosa about it – maybe do an interview with them. Someone gave me your name. Can you call me in New York at 00 1 212 734 8923? Bye for now.

#### Message 3

*Barbara:* This is Barbara Strauss at Autostudio in Hamburg in Germany. We've prepared the drawings you wanted to see, but I can't e-mail them to you, I'm afraid. Can you let me have your fax number? Please phone me on 00 49 40 743 2892. Thank you.

#### Message 4

*Alessandra:* Hi, Melanie. This is Alessandra Tivoli. I'm phoning to say I've heard some very interesting news. It's all top secret! Give me a call at home this evening, and I can tell you all about it. I think you have my number, but here it is, just in case – Modena 34 92 19. Talk to you later.

## Unit 26  KLI are going to buy Mimosa

**26.1** *Silvio:* Good morning, ladies and gentlemen. Welcome to this press conference. My name's Silvio Berio, chairman and chief executive of Mimosa Cars. Let me introduce Johnny Choo, chairman of KL Industries in Malaysia.

*Johnny:* Good morning, everyone.

*Silvio:* Mr Choo has a very important announcement to make. Mr Choo ...

*Johnny:* Yes. KL Industries are going to buy Mimosa Cars ...
Yes, we are the new owners of the company, but Mr Berio is going to stay as chief executive of Mimosa Cars.

**26.2** *Ray:* What are you going to do with Mimosa?

*Johnny:* We're going to invest a lot of money in the company.

*Ray:* How much are you going to invest?

*Johnny:* We're going to spend 500 million euros over the next five years.

*Ray:* What are you going to spend the money on?

*Johnny:* I'm going to replace the older models like the GLX and introduce some new models.

*Ray:* How are you going to develop the engineering side?

*Johnny:* KL Industries are going to give Mimosa a lot of technical help.

### 26.3  On the line

#### Conversation 1

*PA:* Mr Choo's office.

*David:* Can I speak to Mr Choo, please?

*PA:* May I ask who's calling?

*David:* David Lee, chief financial officer at KL Industries in Kuala Lumpur.

*PA:* One moment. I'm putting you through.

*Johnny:* Johnny Choo.

*David:* Johnny, it's David – how are you?

*Johnny:* Fine, David. How are you?

#### Conversation 2

*PA:* Mr Choo's office.

*Ray:* Can I speak to Mr Choo, please?

*PA:* May I ask who's calling?

*Ray:* Ray Baxter, *World Sports Car News*.

*PA:* I'm sorry. Mr Choo isn't available. He's in a meeting.

*Ray:* When's he going to be free?

*PA:* Are you a journalist?

*Ray:* Yes, I am. *World Sports Car News* is a very important magazine.

*PA:* Mr Choo has said that all journalists must call our public relations firm in Milan. Please could you call this number – 02 983 4520.

*Ray:* 02 983 4520. Sure. Thanks for your help.

*PA:* You're welcome. Bye.

*Ray:* Bye.

#### Conversation 3

*PA:* Mr Choo's office.

*Melanie:* Can I speak to Mr Choo, please?

*PA:* May I ask who's calling?

*Melanie:* My name's Melanie Taylor. I'm a senior designer in the design department.

*PA:* I'm sorry. Mr Choo isn't in his office.

*Melanie:* When's he going to be back?

*PA:* Tomorrow morning.

*Melanie:* OK. Thanks very much.

## Unit 27  Have you ever been to Malaysia?

**27.1** *Melanie:* Hi, Paolo – is there anyone sitting here?

*Paolo:* No. Take a seat.

*Melanie:* So, what's the latest news on KL Industries' plans for Mimosa?

*Paolo:* It's looking very good. They're putting a lot of money into the company, as they promised. And we're beginning to work together on the engineering side.

*Melanie:* Good!

*Paolo:* Yes. In fact I'm going to Kuala Lumpur soon to see one of their production engineers, Saleem Bashir. He was here in Modena recently.

*Melanie:* Yes, I met him. Nice guy!

*Paolo:* Yes. I'm looking forward to the trip.

*Melanie:* Have you ever been to Malaysia before?

*Paolo:* No. I've never been to Malaysia, but I've been to Singapore.

## Unit 28  You don't have to wear a jacket

**28.1  On the line**

*Saleem:* Bashir.

*Paolo:* Saleem, hello – it's Paolo Ponte. I'm at Kuala Lumpur airport.

*Saleem:* Welcome to Malaysia! I sent my driver to pick you up. Is he there?

*Paolo:* No, he isn't.

*Saleem:* I'm sorry about that. There's been a mix-up.

*Paolo:* You got my e-mail about the change in the arrival time?

*Saleem:* Yes, and I asked my PA to tell my driver. But my driver got the wrong information and went to the airport this morning.

*Paolo:* Oh, no.

*Saleem:* When you didn't arrive, he came back here. I told him to go out to the airport again. He's on his way now.

*Paolo:* OK. I'll wait for him here.

*Saleem:* Right. Shall we have dinner together this evening?

*Paolo:* Yes, I'd like that.

*Saleem:* I'll meet you at your hotel at about 9 if that's OK.

*Paolo:* That sounds good.

*Saleem:* OK. See you later.

*Paolo:* Bye for now.

## Unit 29  Welcome to the hotel

**29.1**
1 Check in at reception.

2 Go up to the 19th floor and go into your room.

3 Turn on the lights.

4 Put your money in the safe.

5 Take a drink out of the minibar.

6 The air-conditioning is on: if you're hot, turn it up.

7 Go to sleep and wake up.

8 Pick up the phone and order breakfast.

9 From the 19th floor, take the lift down to reception.

10 Check out of the hotel.

**29.2**
*Saleem:* Paolo, good to see you at last. How are you?

*Paolo:* Fine. It's good to be here.

*Saleem:* Sorry I'm late.

*Paolo:* That's all right. Actually, I was rather tired after my flight, so I slept for a couple of hours.

*Saleem:* Good. How do you like Kuala Lumpur?

*Paolo:* It's so hot. I'm glad the air-conditioning in my room works well!

*Saleem:* Yes … So … let's go up to the restaurant on the top floor and eat!

*Paolo:* Right …

*Saleem:* So, what's the latest at Mimosa?

*Paolo:* Well, everyone's very excited about the future … the new models, the new markets …

*Saleem:* There's a lot of work to do, of course.

*Paolo:* Of course.

*Saleem:* Tomorrow we can go to our plant outside Kuala Lumpur. You can meet some of our key people.

*Paolo:* I'm looking forward to that. I'm really interested in your production methods.

*Saleem:* And on Saturday, we can go for a drive if you like. It's good to get out of Kuala Lumpur at weekends. You must see something of Malaysia while you're here.

*Paolo:* Good idea!

## Unit 30  It will be a big success

**30.1**
*Melanie:* So, Paolo – did you have a good trip to Malaysia?

*Paolo:* Yes, it was very useful. Saleem Bashir was very helpful. I had a very good time.

*Melanie:* Good.

*Paolo:* How's it going in the design department?

*Melanie:* The design stage for the GLX mark 2 project is going well. The final design will be complete at the end of June. We're on schedule at the moment.

*Paolo:* Excellent. Adriana, what about the marketing?

*Adriana:* We're talking to different advertising agencies, and we'll choose one by the end of the year.

*Paolo:* Right.

*Adriana:* We'll start the advertising at the beginning of September next year.

*Paolo:* Good! On the production side, we'll start producing the GLX mark 2 in April next year.

*Adriana:* Sounds great! I hope we don't get behind schedule!

*Paolo:* Of course we won't.

*Melanie:* I'm sure we won't …

# Answer key

## 1 Where are you from?

**Listening and speaking**

**A** **3** I'm
**4** my name's
**5** name's
**6** I'm

**B** **2** Sven Karlsson, from
**3** Saleem Bashir, I'm

**C** **a**2 **b**3 **c**1

**Grammar**

**A** I'm (I am) from Malaysia.
You're (You are) from Italy.
He's (He is) from France.
She's (She is) from Brazil.
We're (We are) from America.
You're (You are) from Sweden.
They're (They are) from Poland.

## 2 I'm a designer

**Listening and speaking**

**A** **A:** Where's Fiona from?
**B:** She's from Scotland.
**A:** What's her job?
**B:** She's a designer.

**C** Alessandra Tivoli is from Italy. She's a designer at Mimosa Cars.
Sven Karlsson is from Sweden. He's a sales manager at Splash Pools.
Saleem Bashir is from Malaysia. He's an engineer at KL Industries.
Astrid Schmidt is from Germany. She's a director at Supersport.

**Grammar 1**

**A** **2** a
**3** an
**4** a
**5** a
**6** a

**Grammar 2**

**A** **1** I        my
you      your
he       his
she      her
it       its
we       our
they     their

**B** **2** his
**3** his
**4** your
**5** your

**ON THE LINE** **A** **Melanie:** Is Alessandra Tivoli there?
**Alessandra:** Yes, speaking.
**Melanie:** Hello, Alessandra. This is Melanie.
**Alessandra:** Hello, Melanie.

## 3 How many showrooms?

**Reading** **B** **1** showrooms: 14   employees: 120
**2** offices: 1   showrooms: 3   employees: 25

**Grammar 1** *be* **negative and question forms**

**A** Are you from Argentina?   No, I'm not. I'm from Chile.
Is he from Australia?   No, he isn't. He's from New Zealand.
Is she from France?   No, she isn't. She's from Belgium.
Are you from Japan?   No, we aren't. We're from Korea.
Are they from Egypt?   No, they aren't. They're from Tunisia.

**Grammar 2** **A** **2** Is, isn't
**3** Is, isn't
**4** are, are
**5** many

**Numbers** **A** 0
10
1 11
2 12 20
3 13 30
4 14 40
5 15 50
6 16 60
7 17 70
8 18 80
9 19 90
100

**B** (13) 30 (14) 40 15 (50)
(16) 60 17 (70) 18 (80) (19) (90)
(100) (125) 200 271 (333) (389) 403 (499)

**C** **2** 7       up
**3** Heinz   57 varieties
**4** Peugeot   406
**5** Boeing   747

**ON THE LINE** **A** **A:** Hello.
**B:** Is that Splash Pools?
**A:** Yes, it is.
**B:** Can I speak to Sven Karlsson, please?
**A:** Who's calling?

## 4 We make cars

**Reading**

**B** 2 KL Industries has its headquarters in Kuala Lumpur.

3 There are 200 offices.

4 About 500 employees work there.

5 The offices are very nice, and the furniture is very modern.

6 Parking is easy.

7 At lunchtime, people go shopping.

**Grammar**

**A** Saleem works for KL Industries.

He manages a car factory.

He lives in Kuala Lumpur.

He likes his job.

He loves cars.

**C** Do you speak English?  Yes, I do.

Do you work in an office?  Yes, I do.

Do you sell things?  No, I don't.

Do you manage people?  Yes, I do.

Do you like your job?  Yes, I do.

**E** 2d  3e  4b  5a

**Listening**

**A** **a** h j k

**b** c d e g p t v

**f** l m n s x z

**i** y

**o**

**q** u w

**r**

**ON THE LINE**

**A** 1 Ray Baxter, 001 212 734 8923

2 Paolo Ponte, paolo.ponte@mimosa.it

**B** **PA:** Hello. Mr Bashir's personal assistant.

**Ray:** Hello. Can I speak to Mr Bashir, please?

**PA:** Who's calling?

**Ray:** This is Ray Baxter in New York.

**PA:** I'm sorry, but Mr Bashir isn't here today.

**Ray:** Can he call me tomorrow, please?

## 5 She goes to Spain

**Reading**

**B** 2F  3T  4F  5T  6T

**Grammar**

**A** Does he take a break in August?  No, he doesn't.

Does she go to Spain or Italy?  Yes, she does.

Does it leave at 10.15?  No, it doesn't.

He doesn't take a break in August. He takes a break in July.

She doesn't go to France. She goes to Spain or Italy.

It doesn't leave at 10.15. It leaves at 11.15.

**C** **2 A:** Does she go to Portugal in August?
**B:** No, she goes to Spain or Italy in July.

**3 A:** Does she go skiing in the winter?
**B:** Yes, she does.

**4 A:** Does she go skiing in the Pyrenees?
**B:** No, she goes skiing in the Alps.

**5 A:** Does she stay in Frankfurt at weekends?
**B:** No, she goes to her house in the country.

**Listening** **A** **b** It's eight forty-five.
It's a quarter to nine.

**c** It's nine o'clock.

**d** It's nine fifteen.
It's a quarter past nine.

**e** It's nine twenty-five.
It's twenty-five past nine.

**f** It's nine forty.
It's twenty to ten.

**g** It's ten o'clock.

**h** It's ten oh five.
It's five past ten.

**ON THE LINE** **A** 

| What time is it? | Where is Astrid? | Where is Julia? |
|---|---|---|
| **1** 9.15 am | **1** At the check-in desk at the airport | **1** At the hotel entrance |
| **2** 9.45 am | **2** At the café in the airport | **2** About 5 km from the airport |
| **3** 10.05 am | **3** At the departure gate | **3** About 2 km from the airport |

## 6 How do you relax?

**Reading** **B** **2** eat out

**3** go to the cinema

**4** watch baseball on television

**Listening and speaking** **A**

| NAME: John Baker | | | |
|---|---|---|---|
| **Do you play:**<br>Where:<br>When: | soccer ✓<br>in the park<br>on the weekend | hockey | baseball |
| **Do you go:**<br>Where:<br>When: | walking | camping ✓<br>Rocky Mountains<br>on the weeekend | skiing ✓<br>Lake Tahoe<br>on the weekend |
| OTHER MEMBER OF FAMILY | | | |
| NAME: Jason | | | |
| **Does he/she play:**<br>Where:<br>When: | soccer ✓<br>at school<br>in the evening | hockey | baseball |
| **Does he/she go:**<br>Where:<br>When: | walking | camping ✓<br>Rocky Mountains<br>on the weeekend | skiing ✓<br>Lake Tahoe<br>on the weekend |

**Grammar** **A** **2** When do you play football?

**3** Where do you play?

**4** Who do you play with?

**5** How often do you win?

**6** Why do you play football and not hockey?

**B** **b**7   **c**4   **d**5   **e**6   **f**3

## ☎ ON THE LINE

**A** Park       opens:      closes:
             10.00 am      9.00 pm

**Restaurant**    opens:      last meal:
             11.30 am      8.00 pm

**Ghost train**   first train leaves:    last train leaves:
             10.30 am      6.30 pm

**Cinema**    first film show starts:    last film show starts:
             2.30 pm      7.15 pm

## Review 1–6

**A**   2a   3d   4c   5g   6b   7f

**B**   2a   3c   4b

**C**   **2** In this building there are 50 offices.

      **3** An accountant works in this office.

      **4** There is a special office for the designers.

      **5** There isn't a company restaurant.

      **6** There is a car park for 200 cars.

**D**

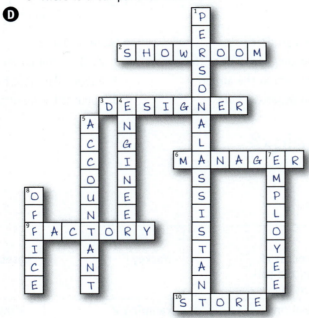

**E**

| | DEPARTURES | TO | GATE |
|---|---|---|---|
| **1** | RG 993 | Rio | 44 |
| **2** | AZ 728 | Rome | 12 |
| **3** | VS 223 | London | 9 |
| **4** | NW 616 | Los Angeles | 26 |
| **5** | SA 821 | Cape Town | 31 |
| **6** | JM 832 | Kingston | 17 |

**H**

| | lives in | works at |
|---|---|---|
| Anita | Montreal | Xenon |
| Ben | Halifax | Walters |
| Chris | Toronto | Zetters |
| Delia | Vacouver | Youngs |

**I**   a11   b1   c5   d9   e7   f3   g12   h6   i2   j8   k10   l4

# 7 We get a lot of visitors

**Reading** **B** 2a  3d  4b  5c

**Grammar** **A** 2 **A:** How many, there

3 **A:** lot

4 **A:** many, do you

5 **A:** How many, do you

**Vocabulary and expressions** **A** Monday, Tuesday, Wednesday, Thursday, Friday

Saturday + Sunday = the weekend

yesterday ← today → tomorrow

 **A** 2T  3F  4F  5T  6T  7F

# 8 Turn left at the lights

**Reading and vocabulary** **A** 2 crossroads

3 tube station

4 corner

5 traffic lights

6 bridge

7 side street

**ON THE LINE** **A** D

**Listening and speaking** **A** 1 **A:** Tea?

**B:** Yes, please.

**A:** Sugar?

**B:** Two, please.

**A:** Here you are.

**B:** Thanks.

2 **A:** Would you like a coffee?

**B:** Yes, please.

**A:** How do you like it?

**B:** White, one sugar, please.

**A:** Here you are.

**B:** Thanks.

3 **A:** Would you like some juice?

**B:** No, thanks.

**A:** Sure?

**B:** I'm OK, thanks.

**B** 2F  3F  4T  5F

# 9 Can I help you?

**Vocabulary** **A** 2e  3b  4a  5c  6g  7f

2e  3d  4a  5b

**Grammar** **C** 2e  3d  4a  5f  6c

**ON THE LINE** **A**

| | |
|---|---|
| product: | indoor saunas |
| number: | 20 |
| colours: | blue, white |
| delivery: | 10 next month, 10 the month after |
| price: | £5,000 |
| normal discount: | 10% |
| discount for this customer: | 12% |

**Writing** **A**
2 white
3 black
4 £6,000
5 12%
6 next month

# 10 I'm buying a house

**Reading** **B** 2T  3T  4T  5F

**Grammar** **A**
I'm (I am) planning the garden now.
You're (You are) planning the garden now.
He's/She's (He/She is) planning the garden now.
We're (We are) planning the garden now.
You're (You are) planning the garden now.
They're (They are) planning the garden now.

Is she looking for a sauna?  No, she isn't looking for a sauna. She's looking for a Jacuzzi.

Are you hoping to buy it soon?  Yes, we are. We're hoping to buy it this week.
Are they moving into the house today?  No, they aren't.

**Listening and speaking** **A** 2a  3d  4c

**ON THE LINE** **A**

| Receptionist | Caller |
|---|---|
| Who's calling, please? | Is that ... ? |
| Unfortunately he's/she's ... | I'm phoning about ... |
| Can I take a message? | Can you give him/her a message? |
| Can I ask him/her to call you back? | Can you ask him/her to call me back? |
| Does he/she have your number? | |

# 11 What's Sven doing?

**Reading**  **B**  **1** It's from Carole Bruckner.
**2** It's 29th October.
**3** It's to Sven Karlsson.
**4** It's about Carole's order for saunas.
**5** She wants to know where the saunas are.

**ON THE LINE**  **A**  2T  3F  4T  5T

**Grammar**  **A**  What's (What is) Sven doing?
Where's he playing?
When's he playing?
Who's he playing?
Why's he playing?
How's he playing?

**Vocabulary**  **A**

| Say | Write |
|---|---|
| the first of May or May the first | 1st May or May 1st |
| the second of May or May the second | 2nd May or May 2nd |
| the third of May or May the third | 3rd May or May 3rd |
| the fourth of May or May the foourth | 4th May or May 4th |
| the fifth of May or May the fifth | 5th May or May 5th |

# 12 The truck's leaving now

**Vocabulary**  **A**  2a  3d  4b

**B**  2T  3F  4T  5T  6F

**C**  Splash Pools

Swedesaunas make saunas at their factory in Kalmar, Sweden. They deliver to customers all over the world. Splash Pools are one of their customers in the UK.

Swedesaunas get an order from Splash Pools for some saunas. They put the saunas on a truck. The truck goes to Gothenburg and drives onto the ferry. The ferry leaves in the evening. It crosses the North Sea and arrives in Harwich the next day. The truck drives off the ferry.

The truck goes to the Swedesaunas warehouse near London. From the warehouse, another truck delivers the saunas to the Splash Pools' showroom in south London, or directly to Splash Pools' customers.

The delivery usually takes two to three days.

**ON THE LINE**  **A**  Apologies

(Please accept) our apologies for the delay/inconvenience.
We're (very) sorry about ...
We're doing everything we can to solve the problem.

Accepting apologies

I accept your apologies.
That's all right.
No problem.

**Writing**  **A**  Model answer

Dear Carole,

Following our phone call, this is to confirm that we are delivering your saunas today. Please accept our apologies for this late delivery.

Best wishes,

Sven Karlsson

# Review 7–12

**A** 2b  3a  4a  5a  6b

**B**  2 Bob is playing golf.

3 Consuelo is sitting in the sauna.

4 Daniel and Ella are talking to customers in the showroom.

5 Fabrizio is swimming in the pool.

6 Georgina is looking at new products.

7 Harold and Laura are waiting for a delivery.

**C**  2 Is Bob playing golf?

3 Is Consuelo sitting in the sauna?

4 Are Daniel and Ella talking to customers in the showroom?

5 Is Fabrizio swimming in the pool?

6 Is Georgina looking at new products?

7 Are Harold and Laura waiting for a delivery?

**D**  2 has

3 work

4 make

5 get

6 take

7 is getting

8 are talking

9 are working

10 are having

11 are leaving

**E**  1 a5  b1  c2  d3  e6  f4

2 a4  b5  c6  d2  e1  f3

3 a3  b1  c2  d4  e6  f5

**G**

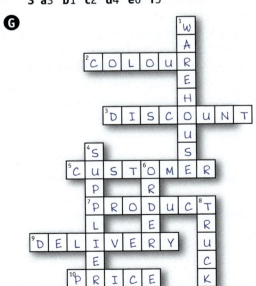

# 13 I work from home

**Reading**  (A) **2** She lives in the south of France.

**3** She likes it because it's so quiet.

**4** She's a designer.

**5** He's a maths teacher.

**6** They go to school in the village.

**Expressions**  (A) **2** leaves for

**3** gets to

**4** at work

**5** off

**6** goes, gets

**7** works, at

**Grammar**  (A)  **2** 8.30

**3** 9

**4** 5.30

**5** 6

**6** 12

**7** 2.30

**8** 1

**9** 4

**10** 7

**11** 8

**ON THE LINE** (A) first name: Douglas      departure date: 10th June
surname: Macpherson      departure time: 2.00 pm
make of car: Renault      payment amount: £254
model of car: Laguna      payment method: Cheque/credit card
number: X168 SNT      type of card: Visa
no. of adults: 2 children: 2      card no.: 1068 068 4599 3427 2846

(B) **Cheryl:**    So, to check the details. Your surname is Macpherson: M-A-C-P-H-E-R-S-O-N.

**Douglas:**  That's right.

**Cheryl:**    You're travelling with a Renault Laguna – two adults, two children, on the 10th of June at 2 pm.

**Douglas:**  Right.

**Cheryl:**    The number of the car is X168 SNT.

**Douglas:**  Correct.

**Cheryl:**    And you're paying by Visa, card number 1068 ...

# 14 We're arriving on Monday

**Grammar 1**  (A) **2** They're stopping in York and Versailles.

**3** They're staying at a hotel.

**4** They're staying at a hotel.

**5** They're arriving on Monday evening.

**Reading and speaking**  (A) Douglas and family are arriving on Monday evening, not Tuesday evening.

(B) **2** working

**3** arriving

**4** I'm

**5** working

**6** meeting

**Grammar 2**  **A** man — men
woman — women
child — children
person — people
family — families
diary — diaries
box — boxes
watch — watches

**ON THE LINE**  **A**

| | |
|---|---|
| **Date of reservation** | 10th June |
| **Number of rooms** | 2 |
| **Number of nights** | 1 |
| **Number of people** | 2 adults, 2 children |
| **Price per room** | 120 euros/€120 |
| **Time of arrival** | 8 pm |

# 15 Can we order, please?

**Listening and speaking**  **A** **Conversations 1a and 1b:** photo C
**Conversations 2a and 2b:** photo A
**Conversations 3a and 3b:** photo B
More polite – 1a, 2a, 3a

**C** 2a  3b  4d  5e  6c

**Reading and vocabulary**  **B** 2 early
3 uncomfortable
4 open
5 cancelled

**Grammar**  **A** I/He/She/It was on time.
We/You/They were on time.
Was I/he/she/it busy?
Were we/you/they busy?
I/He/She/It wasn't comfortable.
We/You/They weren't comfortable.

**ON THE LINE**  **A** The ferry was cancelled.
The restaurant wasn't very good/was terrible.
The hotel was very comfortable.

# 16 I decided to move to France

**Reading**  **B** 2T  3F  4T  5F  6T  7T  8F

**Grammar**  **A** like — liked
move — moved
decide — decided
need — needed
buy — bought
do — did
have — had
go — went

**C**   **1** grew up, didn't stay
    **2** studied, didn't want
    **3** got, didn't like
    **4** worked, didn't feel
    **5** bought, didn't move

    **2** Did she go to a design school in Glasgow?
    **3** Did she work from home for four years?
    **4** Did she move to a big city in France?
    **5** Did she buy a house in the Alps?
    **6** Did she know the Pyrenees before she moved there?

**Listening and speaking**   **A**   **2**c   **3**b   **4**a

## 17 Did you get my message?

**Reading**   **B**   **2**F   **3**F   **4**T   **5**T

**Listening**   **A**   **2**d   **3**b   **4**a

**ON THE LINE**   **A**   **1** Yes, she did.
    **2** Yes, she did.
    **3** No, she didn't.
    **4** No, she didn't. She needs more time.
    **5** They agree that Fiona can work on the designs during the weekend and send them next week.

**Writing**   **A**   **2** send
    **3** got
    **4** hope
    **5** like
    **6** coming
    **7** can
    **8** looking
    **9** hearing

**Reading and speaking**   **B**   **a**7   **b**9   **c**5   **d**3   **e**10   **f**8   **g**4   **h**6

## 18 Where did you go?

**Listening**   **A**   **2** $2\frac{1}{2}$
    **3** juice
    **4** cover
    **5** book

**Grammar**   **A**   **2** How
    **3** Who
    **4** Why
    **5** How long
    **6** What
    **7** When

**ON THE LINE**   **A**   **2** I didn't agree to write the text. / Someone else is writing the text.
    **3** 2 months
    **4** 5

**Writing**   **A** **4** are

**5** is

**6** is

**7** is doing

**8** am sending

**9** can

## Review 13–18

**A** **4** He's at work all day.

**5** He's never ill, so he's never off work.

**6** He gets home in the evening at about 6.00.

**7** His wife Anna works from home.

**8** She's at home in the morning and she goes out in the afternoon for a walk.

**9** She gets home from her walk at 4.30.

**B** **2** doesn't phone, writes

**3** talk

**4** finishes

**5** doesn't work, visits

**6** doesn't like

**7** teaches

**8** go/don't go

**D** **2** had

**3** went

**4** talked

**5** liked

**6** asked

**7** had

**8** ate

**9** drove

**10** felt

**E**
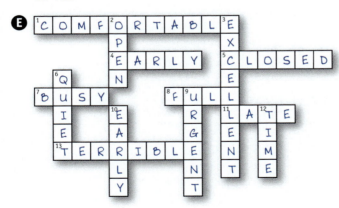

## 19 Supersport has arrived

**Reading**  **B** 2T  3F  4T  5F  6T

**Grammar**  **A** 2 have invested
3 have built
4 have made

**B** arrive      arrived
invest      invested
move        moved
build        built
make         made
sell          sold

**Vocabulary**  **A** 2e  3a  4c  5d

**ON THE LINE**  **A** 21  33  42

## 20 Do you have any tents?

**Vocabulary**  **B** 2 Alamo
3 Bute, McKinley
4 value

**Listening**  **A**

| BIKES | TENTS | JACKETS | BOOTS | MAPS |
|---|---|---|---|---|
| Armstrong  yes<br>Lemond     no | Alamo  no<br>Bute    yes | X500  yes<br>X600 no | Austrian  yes<br>Italian    yes | Colombia  no<br>Ecuador    yes |

**Grammar**  **B**

|  | affirmative | negative | questions | offers |
|---|---|---|---|---|
| *some* | We have some maps of Ecuador. |  |  | Would you like some coffee? |
| *any* |  | We don't have any Italian boots.<br>There aren't any Alamo tents. | Do you have any X500 jackets?<br>Are there any American boots in stock? |  |

**C** 2 any
3 some, any
4 some, any
5 some, any

**ON THE LINE**  **A**

| 1 bikes | 2 tents | 3 jackets | 4 maps |
|---|---|---|---|
| Simpson 8<br>Anquetil 0 | McKinley 0<br>Ogden    1 | X300  0<br>X400  12 | Brazil  20<br>Peru    0 |

**B** b3  c4  d3  e1

# 21 The service was slow

**Listening and speaking**

**A** **Service**

excellent

slow 3

poor

unhelpful

unfriendly 1

good

fast

helpful 2

friendly 4

**Reading and vocabulary**

**B** 2 She works at Rapid Research.

3 870 people spoke to the researchers.

4 650 customers completed questionnaires.

5 She's Lola Fernandez's assistant.

6 He can get in touch with Lola or Linda.

**C** <u>600</u>  <u>650</u>  692  <u>700</u>  <u>738</u>  <u>777</u>  787  <u>792</u>

<u>800</u>  <u>821</u>  843  <u>870</u>  <u>900</u>  950  <u>963</u>  <u>999</u>

**ON THE LINE** **A**

| Supersport customer satisfaction report | | | | |
|---|---|---|---|---|
| | **excellent** | **good** | **fair** | **poor** |
| Quality of products | 35% | 45% | 15% | 5% |
| Choice of products | 40% | 33% | 17% | 10% |
| Availability of products | 9% | 18% | 44% | 29% |

**Reading**

# 22 The smallest company

**B**

| | **Supersport** | **Sportmart** | **Aktiv** |
|---|---|---|---|
| stores | 10 | 25 | 110 |
| employees | 450 | 900 | 3,000 |
| sales last year | $250 million | $700 million | $2 billion |
| profit/loss last year | $5 million loss | $60 million profit | $200 million profit |

**Grammar**

**A**

| comparative | superlative |
|---|---|
| bigger, smaller | biggest, smallest |
| more expensive, more profitable | most expensive, most profitable |
| better | best |
| worse | worst |

**B** 2 Sportmart has higher sales than Supersport, but Aktiv has the highest sales.

3 Sportmart is more profitable than Supersport, but Aktiv is the most profitable company.

**Numbers**

**A** <u>a thousand</u>  10,000  <u>93,000</u>  250,000  <u>€800,000</u>

<u>a million</u>  <u>$5 million</u>  17 million  <u>70 million</u>  <u>278 million</u>

<u>7 billion</u>  <u>$21 billion</u>  54 billion  <u>87 billion</u>  <u>$500 billion</u>

**B** 2c  3b  4a  5f  6d

**C** 1 millions  2 thousands  3 billions

# 23 You must improve training

**Reading**

**B** 4 The look of the store

3 Service problems

1 Quality and choice of products

**C** Stock problems

**ON THE LINE** **A** Astrid wants to meet Harry in Sacramento, not in Los Angeles.

Astrid wants to get a taxi from the airport to Supersport. She doesn't want someone to meet her.

She wants a hotel for two nights, not three.

She wants to stay in the city centre.

**Writing**

**A** **Model answer**

Astrid,

It was good to talk with you. This is to confirm the arrangements for our meeting on Tuesday at 12.00 in Sacramento. I've asked my PA to reserve a hotel for you for two nights. The hotel is in the city centre.

Best wishes,

Harry

**Listening and speaking**

**A**

| | | | |
|---|---|---|---|
| 3 | But | 19 | must |
| 4 | 's | 20 | the |
| 5 | this | 21 | is |
| 6 | are | 22 | aren't |
| 7 | people | 23 | the |
| 8 | buying | 24 | to |
| 9 | our | 25 | who |
| 10 | have | 26 | about |
| 11 | that | 27 | must |
| 12 | are | 28 | and |
| 13 | don't order | 29 | better |
| 14 | on | 30 | don't agree |
| 15 | isn't | 31 | we |
| 16 | in | 32 | the |
| 17 | the | 33 | that |
| 18 | in | | |

# 24 Follow my advice

**Reading**

**B** 2 She advised Harry to improve staff training.

3 No, he didn't.

4 He wants to increase pay to get better employees.

5 No, she doesn't.

6 Astrid is going to talk to the computer systems manager.

**Grammar**

**B** 2 Harry disagreed with her.

3 Astrid told him to keep pay the same.

4 Astrid wants the computer systems manager to phone her.

5 She asked him to go to Sacramento.

**ON THE LINE** **A** a11  b5  c9  d1  e3  f15  g13  h7  i14  j12  k6  l8  m4  n10  o2

**Writing** **A** **Supersport in the US**

3 had

4 is working

5 asked

6 to go

7 am

8 advise

9 to think

# Review 19–24

**A** 2 30,000 people have found jobs this month.

3 The Australian dollar has risen to €1.25.

4 A 20-year-old pilot has flown alone round the world in a small plane.

5 Brazil has/have beaten England 2–1.

6 A man has won €10 million at a/the Monte Carlo casino.

7 Disney has/have announced a new park in Spain.

**B** 2a 3b 4e 5d 6h 7f 8g

**C** 2T 3T 4T 5T 6T 7T 8T 9F 10T

**D** The Utah costs twenty-two thousand two hundred dollars. World sales last year were two hundred and forty-four thousand.

The Virginia costs twenty-five thousand dollars. World sales last year were one hundred and eighty-three thousand.

The Wisconsin costs nineteen thousand five hundred dollars. World sales last year were one hundred and twenty-two thousand.

**E** 2 listen

3 go

4 see

5 pay

6 do

**F**

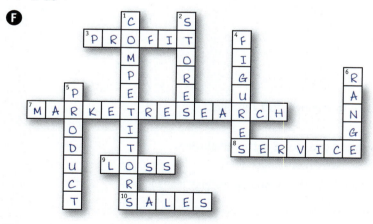

**G** 1 I agree with you about this problem.

2 She told me to leave.

3 I advised him to see a doctor.

4 She wanted us to change the way we work.

5 We disagreed with her.

**H** 2 How about Tuesday next week at 12 noon instead?

3 I'm sorry about this change of day and time.

4 I'm looking forward to our meeting.

5 Best wishes / Best regards

# 25 Don't drive too fast!

**Reading** **B** 2F  3T  4F  5T  6F

**Grammar** **A** **Adverb**

quickly    slowly

easily    happily

early    late    fast    hard

well

**B** 2 rapidly, clearly

3 early, hard, late

4 happily

5 usually

## ON THE LINE **A**

| | | reason | number to call |
|---|---|---|---|
| 1 | Jong-Hun Park | He's visiting Modena on Tuesday. He wants to meet Melanie for lunch. | 00 33 1 78 32 45 61 |
| 2 | Ray Baxter | He wants to talk to a designer at Mimosa about the company, maybe do an interview with them. | 00 1 212 734 8923 |
| 3 | Barbara Strauss | They have prepared drawings that Melanie wanted, but she can't e-mail them. She wants Melanie's fax number. | 00 49 40 743 2892 |
| 4 | Alessandra Tivoli | She has heard some very interesting news. She wants Melanie to phone her at home to talk about it. | Modena 34 92 19 |

# 26 KLI are going to buy Mimosa

**Vocabulary** **A** 2 chief executive

3 chief financial officer

4 head of production

5 chief designer

6 marketing director

**Listening** **A** 1 Two

2 Silvio Berio and Johnny Choo

3 b

**Grammar** **A** 2 How much are you going to invest?

– We're going to spend 500 million euros over the next five years.

3 What are you going to spend the money on?

– I'm going to replace the older models like the GLX and introduce some new models.

4 How are you going to develop the engineering side?

– KL Industries are going to give Mimosa a lot of technical help.

## ON THE LINE

**A**
1 David Lee. She puts him through.
2 Ray Baxter. She doesn't put him through.
3 Malanie Taylor. She doesn't put her through.

**B** conversations:

| | 1 | 2 | 3 |
|---|---|---|---|
| *May I ask who's calling?* | ✓ | ✓ | ✓ |
| *I'm putting you through.* | ✓ | | |
| *Mr Choo isn't available.* | | ✓ | |
| *He's in a meeting.* | | ✓ | |
| *Mr Choo isn't in his office.* | | | ✓ |
| *Please could you call ...* | | ✓ | |

# 27 Have you ever been to Malaysia?

**Reading**

**B**
2 Yes, the trip was useful – he learnt a lot.
3 He wants to invite Paolo to visit Malaysia.
4 He wants to show him the KL Industries factory.
5 He suggests three days.
6 No, he isn't.

**Grammar**

**A**
2 Have you ever been to Sweden?
– No, I've never been to Sweden, but I've been to Norway.
3 Have you ever been to Venice?
– No, I've never been to Venice, but I've been to Rome.
4 Have you ever been to Egypt?
– No, I've never been to Egypt, but I've been to Tunisia.
5 Have you ever been to Johannesburg?
– No, I've never been to Johannesburg, but I've been to Cape Town.

**Writing**

**A**
2 've never been
3 've been
4 hope
5 can
6 've heard
7 is going
8 's going
9 Looking
10 seeing

# Unit 28 You don't have to wear a jacket

**Reading and grammar 1**

**C**
2 mustn't
3 don't have to
4 mustn't
5 don't have to

**D** b

**Grammar 2**

**A** 2a   3e   4c   5d

**ON THE LINE**  **A**  **2** Yes, he did.

**3** Saleem's PA told the driver about the change.

**4** He got the wrong information.

**5** He's on his way back to the airport.

**6** They're going to meet at Paolo's hotel.

## 29 Welcome to the hotel

**Reading and vocabulary**

**B**  **2**d  **3**f  **4**b  **5**a  **6**e

**C**  **2** The Shangrila Restaurant.

**3** The Pool / Power Gym Club and Pool.

**4** 6 pm–2 am

**5** 7–10.30 am

**6** any time

**Grammar**

**A**  **3** on

**4** in

**5** out

**6** up

**7** up

**8** up

**9** down

**10** out

**Listening and speaking**

**B**  **2**F  **3**T  **4**F  **5**T  **6**F  **7**F

**Writing**

**A**  **Model answer**

**3** The visit to the KLI factory was very interesting.

**4** I enjoyed the trip to the coast on Saturday. It was good to see something of Malaysia.

**5** I look forward to working with you on the GLX mark 2.

## 30 It will be a big success

**Reading**

**B**  **2**b  **3**c  **4**a  **5**b  **6**a

**Grammar**

**A**  **2** 'll      2

**3** will    1

**4** will    1

**5** won't  2

**Vocabulary and listening**

**A**  **2** stage

**3** complete

**4** schedule

**5** on schedule

**6** behind schedule

**B**  ✓ behind schedule   ✓ complete   ✓ on schedule   project   ✓ schedule   ✓ stage

**Writing**

**(A)** **3** is going
**4** will complete
**5** is looking
**6** will start
**7** am
**8** will finish
**9** will be

# Review 25–30

**(A)** **2** usually
**3** happily
**4** carefully
**5** terrible, careless
**6** easily
**7** dangerous, careless

**(B)** **2**a **3**b **4**e **5**d

**(C)** **2**a **3**b **4**a **5**a **6**a

**(E)** **2** must
**3** mustn't
**4** don't have to
**5** mustn't
**6** must
**7** must
**8** mustn't

**(F)** **2** down, up
**3** in, out
**4** up, up
**5** up
**6** up

**(G)**

**(H)** **2**e **3**d **4**c **5**a **6**g **7**b

## 31 New markets

**Fax**  **B**

| | | | |
|---|---|---|---|
| 3 | am sending | 9 | will take |
| 4 | you | 10 | will be |
| 5 | sign | 11 | and |
| 6 | and | 12 | not |
| 7 | return | 13 | to |
| 8 | it | | |

**Company description**  **B**  *Lystra* is published by Cosima Publishing Ltd, an international publishing firm based in London, UK. It also has offices in Madrid, Paris and Frankfurt.

There are two editions of the magazine: UK and Europe. There are 800,000 readers worldwide.

*Lystra* comes out weekly.

The magazine deals with fashion and food.

## 32 A big market

**Letter**  **B**  **b**1  **c**5  **d**7  **e**3  **f**4  **g**6

**C**  **2**c  **3**d  **4**a

**Report**  **B**

| | | | |
|---|---|---|---|
| 2 | Region 3 | 8 | $2.50 |
| 3 | 150,000 | 9 | $1.90 |
| 4 | Region 2 | 10 | travel |
| 5 | 100,000 | 11 | fashion |
| 6 | 480,000 | 12 | health |
| 7 | $1.50 | 13 | Region 3 |

## 33 A marketing manager

**Job application**  **B**

| | | | |
|---|---|---|---|
| 3 | in | 13 | speak |
| 4 | to apply | 14 | and |
| 5 | from | 15 | moved |
| 6 | my | 16 | to |
| 7 | have | 17 | for |
| 8 | of | 18 | to |
| 9 | in | 19 | to |
| 10 | a | 20 | forward |
| 11 | in | 21 | from |
| 12 | on | | |

## 34 An interview

**Email exchange**  **B**  **a**4  **b**2  **c**3  **d**6  **e**f  **f**1

**C** Model answer

Thank you for your e-mail. Unfortunately I couldn't open the attachment. Please could you send it again? Many thanks.

Please find attached my résumé again. I hope you can open it this time.

Thanks for sending your résumé again. I can open it now. Can you come for an interview on Monday 10th July?

Unfortunately Monday morning isn't possible for me. I have an important meeting. Is Monday afternoon at 2.00 pm possible?

I'm sorry, but 9.00 am on 10th July is the only possible date and time. I'm leaving for a trip to the Far East at midday.

Fine. I'll change my meeting. I can now come on 10th July at 9.00 am.

**E-mail**

**B** a2  b5  c3  d1  e4

Model answer

Dear Ms Ramsden,

Thank you for offering me the job of Marketing Manager. I accept your proposed salary of $70,000 per year plus bonus. I confirm that I can start on March 1st.

Looking forward to receiving the contract,

Best regards,

Luisa Barcarem

**C** a5  b4  c1  d2  e3

Model answer

Dear Ms Barcarem,

Thanks for your e-mail. I'm sending your contract by FedEx courier today. I'll be in Buenos Aires from March to September to prepare for the September launch of the Latin American edition of *Novina*.

I look forward to seeing you in Buenos Aires on March 1st.

Best regards,

Charlotte Ramsden

# 35 Congratulations!

**Text message**

**B** 1 I got the marketing job in Buenos Aires!

2 Congratulations! When do you start?

3 March 1st. Are you free for dinner tonight?

4 Where do you suggest?

5 How about Carlo's at 7.30 this evening?

6 I forget where it is.

7 It's in University Avenue.

8 OK. See you later!

**Emoticons**

**A** 2g  3f  4h  5b  6e  7d  8a

# 36 You're doing a great job!

**Report** **B**

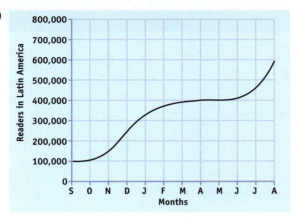

## Review 31–36

**A** Model answer

Dear Sir/Madam,

Please find enclosed an invoice for $25,000. Please note this must be paid within 30 days.

Yours faithfully,

**B** Model answer

Dear Mr Rousseau,

Please find enclosed another copy of our invoice for $25,000. This has still not been paid. Please could you pay this invoice as soon as possible.

If you have any questions, please do not hesitate to contact me.

Yours sincerely,

**C** Dear Francisco,

You said there were 600,000 possible readers in Latin America. We have now reached this target. Your research report was right.

Thank you very much for all your work on it.

We will certainly work with you in the future on new editions.

All best wishes,

Charlotte

**D** 2d 3e 4i 5b 6a 7f 8g 9h 10c

**E** I'm sending this message before I get on the plane. Thanks for a great time in Buenos Aires. Sorry I couldn't stay longer. It'll be difficult to work tomorrow!

Lots of love,

Clarissa

**F** Model answer

110 people work at the *Novina* office in Buenos Aires. The biggest group is from Argentina – there are 65 Argentineans. This is normal, as Buenos Aires is in Argentina! Next comes Brazil, with 11 employees. There are 9 employees from Chile, and 6 each from Colombia and Peru. There are 5 Mexicans and 2 Uruguayans, and 6 people from the rest of South and Central America. This gives a total of 110 people in the *Novina* office.

**G** Model answer

In Year 1, we started with 51 employees. The number rose to 62 in Year 2 and 74 in Year 3. However, this fell to 68 in the following year because there were economic problems in the whole of Latin America, and sales of the magazine fell. But we started to recruit new people in Year 5, when the total number of employees reached 89. This number stayed the same in the following year. There was another increase in Year 7, and there are now 110 employees in the *Novina* office.

# Student B material

## 2  I'm a designer

**ON THE LINE** **B**

**Student B**

Answer three phone calls, You are:
1 Sven Karlsson
2 Saleem Bashir
3 Astrid Schmidt

## 3  How many showrooms?

**Numbers** **D**

**Student B**

Give these numbers when Student A asks for them.
*The number for Splash Pools UK is 020 7627 8790.*

> 1 Splash Pools UK: 020 7627 8790
> 2 Supersport: 069 364 8600
> 3 Mimosa Cars: 059 53 74 21
> 4 KL Industries: 03 2 162 2244

**ON THE LINE** **B**

**Student B**

Answer the phone at these three companies when Student A calls.
1 Supersport
2 Mimosa Cars
3 KL Industries

## 4  We make cars

**ON THE LINE** **C**

**Student B**

You are Alessandra Tivoli, a designer at Mimosa cars in Modena.

- Call KL Industries. You want to speak to Saleem Bashir.
- Give your name.
- Ask: *Can he call me tomorrow about the new machines in the factory?*
- Give your telephone number: 00 39 59 53 74 21
- Give your e-mail address: alessandra.tivoli@mimosa.it

## 6  How do you relax?

**ON THE LINE** **B**

**Student B**

When Student A asks you, tell him/her about the winter programme times.

| Magic World winter programme | | |
| --- | --- | --- |
| **Park** | opens: 11.00 am | closes: 7.45 pm |
| **Restaurant** | opens: 12 noon | last meal: 6.00 pm |
| **Ghost train** | first train leaves: 11.30 am | last train leaves: 4.10 pm |
| **Cinema** | closed | |

# 7  We get a lot of visitors

**Grammar**  **C**

*Student B*

You work in the Splash Pools warehouse. When Student A asks you, talk about the number of products there are.

**A:** *How many indoor saunas are there?*
**B:** *Not many – only three.*

| indoor saunas | 3 |
|---|---|
| outdoor saunas | 45 |
| small Jacuzzis | 67 |
| large Jacuzzis | 1 |

**N THE LINE**  **B**

*Student B*

- Student A asks to meet you at your office. Suggest a day and time for the meeting. *How about ... ?*
- When A suggests another day and time, accept and say *OK. See you on ...day.*
- Say goodbye.

# 8  Turn left at the lights

**N THE LINE**  **B**

*Student B*

You are driving to Splash Pools but you are lost. Make three calls to Splash Pools. Note down the receptionist's directions.

- You are in King's Avenue. *Hello. I'm lost. I'm in King's Avenue. Can you tell me the way to Splash Pools?*
- You are in Long Road.
- You are in Acre Lane.

**Speaking**  **A**

*Student B*

You are a new customer. When Sven asks you, give him the information about the products that you need.

*We need 20 indoor saunas next month.*

|  | number | delivery |
|---|---|---|
| indoor saunas | 20 | next month |
| outdoor saunas | 10 | in three months |
| small Jacuzzis | 25 | in January |
| large Jacuzzis | 15 | in March |

# 9 Can I help you?

ON THE LINE **B**

**Student B**

You are an old customer of Splash Pools. Phone Student A (Sven Karlsson) to place an order.

*Hello, Sven. I'm phoning to place an order for Jacuzzis.*

| product: | indoor Jacuzzis |
|---|---|
| number: | 10 |
| colours: | You want five white and five black. |
| delivery: | You want delivery next month. Can he do this? |
| price: | How much? |
| normal discount: | 10% |
| discount for this customer: | Can he give 12 per cent for an old customer? |

# 10 I'm buying a house

**Listening and speaking** **B**

**Student B**

You are Tania, Sven Karlsson's colleague at Splash Pools. Use this information to answer Sven's questions.

- You are working on an order for a big pool. The customer is spending £20,000.
  *I'm working on an order for a big pool. The customer is spending £20,000.*
- Tell Sven where the other sales reps are:
  Len – on holiday – swimming in the Caribbean
  Cathy – having lunch
  Brian – back from holiday, but he is ill – lying in bed at home.
- Ask Sven how much SSC are spending.
- Offer to work on the SSC order.
- End the conversation.

# 11 What's Sven doing?

**ON THE LINE** **A**

*Student B*

You are Carole Bruckner. You get a call from Tracey, Sven's assistant.

- Listen to what Tracey says. *OK, Right …*
- When Tracey says *You can phone Sven on Monday morning*, say *He can phone me on Monday*. Ask if Sven has your number.
- End the conversation.

**Speaking** **B**

*Student B*

You are Sven Karlsson's assistant, Tracey. Student A plays three visitors to Splash Pools.

**1** Arabella Adams, Monday 1st November, 11 am

**2** Bob Brandt, Tuesday 2nd November, 1.45 pm

**3** Carla Cobb, Wednesday 3rd November, 3.10 pm

- Start the conversations like this:

**A:** *My name's Arabella Adams. Can I see Sven Karlsson, please? I have an appointment with him.*
**B:** *Are you sure?*
**A:** *Yes, it's in my diary. Monday the first of November, 11 o'clock.*

- Check Sven's diary and say what he is doing.

**B:** *I'm sorry, Ms Adams. He's visiting a new customer.*

- Look at the diary below and suggest another time next week. *Can you come back next Tuesday afternoon? How about 4 o'clock?*
- Confirm the date for the new appointment. *So, Tuesday the ninth of November at 4 o'clock.*
- Then say goodbye.

# 12 The truck's leaving now

**ON THE LINE A**

**Student B**

You are Sven. You get two phone calls from Carole Bruckner (Student A).

First phone call: Tuesday

- You receive a call from Carole. *Hello Carole. How can I help you?*
- Use the information in the e-mail below to answer her questions.
- Apologise for the delay and end the conversation.

Second phone call: Thursday

- Carole calls again. *Hello again, Carole.*
- Tell her the delivery truck is coming to Energy Gyms now.
- Apologise for the delay and end the conversation.

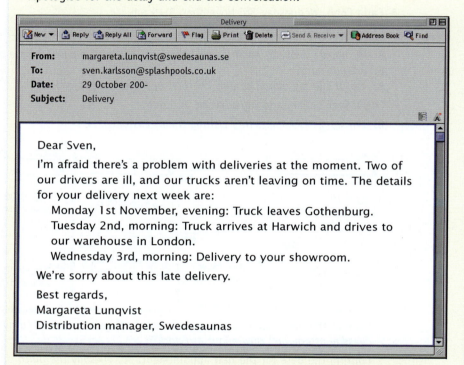

Delivery

New ▾ | Reply | Reply All | Forward | Flag | Print | Delete | Send & Receive ▾ | Address Book | Find

**From:** margareta.lunqvist@swedesaunas.se
**To:** sven.karlsson@splashpools.co.uk
**Date:** 29 October 200-
**Subject:** Delivery

Dear Sven,

I'm afraid there's a problem with deliveries at the moment. Two of our drivers are ill, and our trucks aren't leaving on time. The details for your delivery next week are:

Monday 1st November, evening: Truck leaves Gothenburg.
Tuesday 2nd, morning: Truck arrives at Harwich and drives to our warehouse in London.
Wednesday 3rd, morning: Delivery to your showroom.

We're sorry about this late delivery.

Best regards,
Margareta Lunqvist
Distribution manager, Swedesaunas

## 14 We're arriving on Monday

**☎N THE LINE** **B**

**Student B**

You are James Boyd. Phone the Hotel du Parc. You want to:

- make a reservation for the nights of 10th and 11th December for one person. *I'd like to make a reservation for the nights of the 10th and 11th of December for one person.*
- know the price of the room. *How much / room / cost?*
- know if breakfast is included. */ breakfast included?*
- pay by credit card. *I'd like / pay / credit card (MasterCard 9342 8923 1673 9864)*
- know if the hotel has a car park. *Does / hotel have / car park?*

You are arriving about 9.30 pm.

## 15 Can we order, please?

**☎N THE LINE** **B**

**Student B**

A friend (Student A) is coming to see you from another country. Ask them about:

- the trip. *Was the ferry/plane/train/bus on time?*
- the restaurant yesterday evening. *Was the restaurant good?*
- the hotel last night. *Was the hotel comfortable?*

## 16 I decided to move to France

**Listening and speaking** **B**

**Student B**

You are visiting Student A. You arrive at A's house in the evening. Use these ideas to answer A's questions.

- finding the house / not easy *It wasn't easy to find your house.*
- journey / difficult
- lunch / in a restaurant / excellent
- luggage / five bags

## 17 Did you get my message?

**☎N THE LINE** **B**

**Student B**

You are Amanda Lee-Smith of Pocket Books. Fiona (Student A) phones you about some designs you are waiting for. Ask if she:

- sent the designs. *Did you send the designs?*
- got an e-mail from you. You sent it on Tuesday.
- can send the designs again.

Then end the conversation.

## Review 13–18

**C**

**Student B**

You work for a travel company. You get a call from Student A, who wants to change their ferry reservation.

- Ask about the changes A wants to make and write them down.
- Find the difference between the old price and the new price and ask how they want to pay.
- End the conversation politely.

## 19  Supersport has arrived

**Grammar**  **D**

*Student B*

You are Astrid Schmidt. Student A is a journalist. Answer their questions, using the present perfect forms of the verbs in brackets.

1  Yes. I / (buy) / apartment / Manhattan.
   **A:** *Have you moved to New York?*
   **B:** *Yes. I've bought an apartment in Manhattan.*
2  Yes. I think Supersport / (make) / right decision
3  We / (build) ten stores – nine / New England / one / California
4  Yes. We / (invest) / 400 million dollars
5  No. We / (not open) / too many stores

## 21  The service was slow

**ON THE LINE**  **B**

*Student B*

• You are Lola Fernandez. Use the information in the table to give Harry (Student A) the missing figures for the last two lines – Service and The look of the store.

   **A:** *What are the figures for service?*
   **B:** *15 per cent of customers think the service is excellent, 25 per cent good, 32 per cent fair and 28 per cent poor.*

• End the conversation.

   **A:** *Thanks for your help.*
   **B:** *That's all right.*

**Rapid Research Inc.**

**Supersport customer satisfaction report**

|  | excellent | good | fair | poor |
|---|---|---|---|---|
| Quality of products | 35% | 45% | 15% | 5% |
| Choice of products | 40% | 33% | 17% | 10% |
| Availability of products | 9% | 18% | 44% | 29% |
| Service | 15% | 25% | 32% | 28% |
| The look of the store | 12% | 24% | 48% | 16% |

## 23  You must improve training

**Listening and speaking**  **C**

*Student B*

You are the head of operations for a supermarket chain. Market research shows that there are problems at one of your supermarkets.

• Phone the manager of the supermarket (Student A). Tell him/her that customers think that the store is not clean (floor, shelves, check-outs, etc). *Your customers are saying that the supermarket is dirty.* Tell him/her to check the work of the cleaners better, and sack the bad ones (= tell them to leave). *You must check the work of the cleaners. You must sack the bad ones.*

• Tell the manager that customers think that the check-out staff do not know the products: they have to ask their colleagues, and this slows everything down. Tell him/her to train the check-out staff correctly from their first day of work. (It doesn't matter if they leave.)

• Finish by saying that you are going to visit the supermarket next week.

## 25 Don't drive too fast!

**ON THE LINE** **B**

**Student B**

- You are Alessandra Tivoli. When Melanie Taylor (Student A) asks you what the secret is, tell her that another company is buying Mimosa Cars.

Answer her questions. Use this information:
- An e-mail for Mimosa's boss came to you by mistake.
- The name of the other company is KL Industries.
- You have heard that KL Industries are going to put a lot of money into Mimosa.
- End the conversation.

## 26 KLI are going to buy Mimosa

**ON THE LINE** **C**

**Student B**

You play the people below in three different calls.
- Phone Mimosa and ask Johnny Choo's PA (Student A) if you can speak to Johnny Choo.
- If the assistant doesn't put you through, end the call politely.
- If the assistant puts you through, thank him/her.

1 Gudrun Olafsson, a journalist at *Sports Car Gazette*
2 Paolo Ponte, head of production at Mimosa
3 Elena Zucconi, minister for industry in Italy (you want to thank Mr Choo for investing in Italy)

## 27 Have you ever been to Malaysia?

 **Listening and speaking** **A**

**Student B**

You are Paolo Ponte. Use this information to answer Melanie Taylor's questions.
- Leave: Wednesday at 11 am
  **A:** *When are you leaving?*
  **B:** *I'm leaving on Wednesday at 11 am.*
- Airline: Alitalia *I'm flying on …*
- Change planes: in Rome and again in Bangkok.
- Arrive: Thursday at 11.50 am.
- Coming back on Sunday to give time for some sightseeing! (No need to give all the details about the return flight!)
- Hotel: You don't know. Saleem Bashir is arranging it.

## 28 You don't have to wear a jacket

**ON THE LINE** **B**

**Student B**

You live in Sydney. You get a call from your friend (Student A) who is at Sydney airport.
- Answer the phone.
- You thought your friend's flight arrived at 7 pm.
  *I thought your flight arrived at 7 pm / 7 in the evening.*
- Apologise for the mix-up.
  *Sorry about the mix-up!*
- You are coming to the airport now
- It takes about an hour to get to the airport.
- Apologise again.
- End the conversation.

## Best Practice Elementary Coursebook
*Bill Mascull*

**Publisher:** *Christopher Wenger*
**Director of Product Development:** *Anita Raducanu*
**Director of Marketing:** *Amy Mabley*
**Editorial Manager:** *Howard Middle (HM ELT Services)*
**Intl. Marketing Manager:** *Eric Bredenberg*
**Developmental Editor:** *Louise Elkins*
**Editors:** *Sally Carpenter, Kathy Mestheneou*
**Production Management:** *Oxford Designers & Illustrators*

**Sr. Print Buyer:** *Mary Beth Hennebury*
**Associate Marketing Manager:** *Laura Needham*
**Photo Researchers:** *Billie Porter; Suzanne Williams/ PictureResearch.co.uk*
**Text Designer:** *Oxford Designers & Illustrators*
**Cover Designer:** *Sherman & Dutton*
**Printer:** *Canale & C S.p.A*

For more information contact Thomson Learning, High Holborn House, 50/51 Bedford Row, London WCIR 4LR, United Kingdom or Thomson Heinle, 25 Thomson Place, Boston, Massachusetts 02210, USA. You can visit our Internet site at http://www.heinle.com

For permission to use material from this text or product, submit a request online at http://www.thomsonrights.com

Any additional questions about permissions can be submitted by email to thomsonrights@thomson.com

**ISBN: 1-4130-0902-6**

**Author's acknowledgements:**
The author would like to thank Chris Hartley for his help and support in the initial development of *Best Practice*.

**Acknowledgements:** The publishers and author are grateful to the following teachers for their advice during the development of the book: George Tomaszevski (France), James Tierney, David Massey (Italy), Marina Laso Taylor, Clark Waring (Spain), Manuel Hidalgo Iglesias, Paloma Varela (Mexico), Alicia Carturegli, Marcela S. Rodríguez (Argentina), Alex Chevrolle (China), Forrest Nelson (Japan), Peter Loughran (Hong Kong).

**Illustrations**
Mark Duffin pp 11, 56; all other artwork Oxford Designers & Illustrators

**Photo credits**
The publishers would like to thank the following sources for permission to reproduce their copyright protected photographs:
**Cover Image:** Image Source/Creatas
**Alamy** pp 6br (Image Source), 6tc (BananaStock), 22br (Image Source), 25 (BananaStock), 28 (Elizabeth Whiting & Associates), 38r (Pat Behnke) 42r (Andy Marshall), 042t (Sébastien Baussais), 46 (Paul Shawcross), 78bl (Eric Horan), 78tr (Yadid Levy), 87b (Comstock Images), 91 & 95r & 95tl (*all* Image Source 7), 101 (Pixland); **Axiom** p 87t (David Constantine); **Corbis** pp 7bl (Reuters), 7tc (Shaun/Best Reuters Newmedia Inc), 7tl & 7tr (Reuters), 12l (Tibor Bognar), 14b (Owen Franken), 17 (Robert Landau), 22cl (Paul Souders), 22r (Alen MacWeeney), 54b (Owen Franken), 56b (David Samuel), 62br (Mug Shots), 64 (John Henley Photography), 72 (Chuck Savage), 74r (Sergio Pitamitz), 76 (Yang Liu), 78br (Robert Holmes); **Getty Images** pp 4-5 (Britt Erlanson), 6bc (Photodisc), 6bl & 6tl (Digital Vision), 6tr (AITCH), 8 & 9 (Digital Vision), 12r (Photodisc), 14t (AITCH), 20 (Jack Ambrose), 33 (Terje Rakke), 36-37 (Robert Frerck), 38tl & 39 (Digital Vision), 40 (Jacob Stoch Photography), 49 (Nicolas Russell), 52-3 (Dennis O'Clair), 54tr (AITCH), 58 (Yellow Dog Productions), 68-9 (Andrew Sacks), 77 (Photodisc Red), 80 (Alan Levinson), 84-5 (Lester Lefkowitz), 86r (Photodisc Red), 90 (Chabruken); **Masterfile** pp 22cr (Greg Stott), 42l (Jeremy Woodhouse), 70 (Imtek Engineering); **PA Photos** p 103; **Rex Features** p 24 (Jeroen Oerlemans); Superstock pp 10 & 22l (Raymond Forbes), 30, 41 (Yoshio Tomii), 60